Consumerism in World History

'This is a clever book.' *Business History*

The desire to acquire luxury goods and leisure services is a basic force in modern life. *Consumerism in World History* explores both the historical origins and world-wide appeal of this relatively modern phenomenon. By relating consumerism to other issues in world history, this book forces reassessment of our understanding of both consumerism and global history.

This second edition of *Consumerism in World History* draws on recent research of the consumer experience in the West and Japan, while also examining societies less renowned for consumerism, such as Africa. Every chapter has been updated and new features include:

- a new chapter on Latin America
- Russian and Chinese developments since the 1990s
- the changes involved in trying to bolster consumerism as a response to recent international threats
- examples of consumerist syncretism, as in efforts to blend beauty contests with traditional culture in Kerala.

With updated suggested reading, the second edition of *Consumerism in World History* is essential reading for all students of world history.

Peter N. Stearns is Provost and Professor of History at George Mason University. His books include *The Other Side of Western Civilization* (5th edition, 1999), *Childhood in World History* (Routledge, 2005) and *Gender in World History* (2nd edition, Routledge, 2006).

Themes in World History
Series editor: Peter N. Stearns

The *Themes in World History* series offers focused treatment of a range of human experiences and institutions in the world history context. The purpose is to provide serious, if brief, discussions of important topics as additions to textbook coverage and document collections. The treatments will allow students to probe particular facets of the human story in greater depth than textbook coverage allows, and to gain a fuller sense of historians' analytical methods and debates in the process. Each topic is handled over time – allowing discussions of changes and continuities. Each topic is assessed in terms of a range of different societies and religions – allowing comparisons of relevant similarities and differences. Each book in the series helps readers deal with world history in action, evaluating global contexts as they work through some of the key components of human society and human life.

Gender in World History
Peter N. Stearns

Warfare in World History
Michael S. Neiberg

Disease and Medicine in World History
Sheldon Watts

Western Civilization in World History
Peter N. Stearns

The Indian Ocean in World History
Milo Kearney

Asian Democracy in World History
Alan T. Wood

Revolutions in World History
Michael D. Richards

Migration in World History
Patrick Manning

Sports in World History
David G. McComb

The United States in World History
Edward J. Davies II

Food in World History
Jeffrey M. Pilcher

Alcohol in World History
Gina Hames

Childhood in World History
Peter N. Stearns

Religion in World History
John Super and Briane Turley

Consumerism in World History

The global transformation of desire
Second edition

Peter N. Stearns

Routledge
Taylor & Francis Group

NEW YORK AND LONDON

First published 2001
by Routledge
270 Madison Avenue, New York, NY 10016

Simultaneously published in the UK
by Routledge
2 Park Square, Abingdon, Oxon OX14 4RN

Reprinted 2003, 2004

2nd Edition 2006

Routledge is an imprint of the Taylor & Francis Group

Typeset in Garamond and Gill by
Florence Production Ltd, Stoodleigh, Devon
Printed and bound in Great Britain by
The Cromwell Press, Trowbridge, Wiltshire

Every effort has been made to ensure that the advice and information
in this book is true and accurate at the time of going to press. However,
neither the publisher nor the authors can accept any legal responsibility
or liability for any errors or omissions that may be made. In the case
of drug administration, any medical procedure or the use of technical
equipment mentioned within this book, you are strongly advised to
consult the manufacturer's guidelines.

British Library Cataloguing in Publication Data
A catalogue record for this book is available from the British Library

Library of Congress Cataloging in Publication Data
Stearns, Peter N.
  Consumerism in world history: the global transformation of desire/
  Peter N. Stearns. – 2nd ed.
    p. cm. – (Themes in world history)
    Simultaneously published in the UK. Includes bibliographical
    references and index. I. Consumption (Economics) – History.
    I. Title. II. Series.
    HC79.C6S74 2006
    339.4'7–dc22   2005026759

ISBN10: 0–415–39586–0 (hbk)
ISBN10: 0–415–39587–9 (pbk)

ISBN13: 9–78–0–415–39586–1 (hbk)
ISBN13: 9–78–0–415–39587–8 (pbk)

Contents

Preface

Throughout most of modern history, when a major catastrophe occurred – such as war – people in the society affected were asked to sacrifice some of their consumer pleasures in the interests of the larger good. But when a major terrorist attack hit the United States in September 2001, government leaders hastened to urge people to keep their consumer activities going. Sustaining the economy was more important than sacrifice, and the government proved willing to go into deficit to reconcile anti-terrorism spending with continued consumerist zeal. Some people found the result confusing: if the nation was in peril, shouldn't sacrifice be part of the response? Others accepted the policies but noted the innovation involved. Had consumerism advanced so far that classic responses to disaster now had to be rethought? Were Americans now so dependent on consumerist pleasures that they could not be deprived without possible alienation? The whole episode made several points clear: consumerism is a vital part of modern history; its role continues to change with time; and it remains controversial, generating some sense that it is unnatural or at least inferior to other societal goals.

We live in a world permeated by consumerism, but we rarely step back to examine what this means. Understanding what consumerism means and how it developed historically will allow us a better grasp of a host of international issues and will offer some of us a perspective on ourselves.

Consumerism is best defined by seeing how it emerged, but obviously we need some preliminary sense of what we are talking about. Consumerism describes a society in which many people formulate their goals in life partly through acquiring goods that they clearly do not need for subsistence or for traditional display. They become enmeshed in the process of acquisition – shopping – and take some of their identity from a procession of new items that they buy and exhibit. In this society, a host of institutions both encourage and serve consumerism, from eager shopkeepers trying to lure customers into buying more than they need, to product designers employed to put new twists on established models, to advertisers seeking to create new needs.

A study of consumerism focuses on both sides of the phenomenon: the development of consumer apparatus (the new stores and promotions) and the emergence of the needs and goals from the customer side.

Historical research on consumerism has blossomed in recent years, which is not surprising given the importance of consumer behavior in modern life. For a long time, historical work was constrained by strong beliefs that this was a frivolous topic, unworthy of scholarly attention in comparison with wars or kings or presidents. Elements of this attitude still linger, but on the whole historians have made a successful case for the importance of examining consumerism through the lens of their discipline, precisely because the behavior is so important and because historical perspective is so illuminating. This means that consumerism can now be studied in terms of origins and initial causes, subsequent changes and stages, from its beginnings on to our own times.

One historian – Michael Miller, who wrote a history of one of the first department stores – has argued that consumerism is among the most surprising, the most unexpected developments in modern history, because it involves the most jarring clashes with previous, traditional values. It is a claim worth examining, and this book will contribute to this examination. Would someone transported from the seventeenth century find our consumer expectations and behaviors stranger than our industrial work systems or our political life?

Consumerism has certainly become a field for new historical discovery. Until about a decade ago, it was assumed that consumer society followed from the industrial revolution, thus beginning to emerge only at the end of the nineteenth century. We now know that, while there was a new surge around 1900, modern consumerism predates the industrial revolution. And it was born in Western Europe, with the United States coming on board only as an imitator, even though the nation would ultimately develop a world lead in some facets of consumer standards.

This book, which takes the newest research as its point of departure, rests on several assumptions, which of course need to be tested in the chapters to come, and not just stated here. First, as already indicated, is the belief that consumerism is extremely important and that it can be explored historically with profit.

Second is the argument that consumerism, as it came to apply to various social levels, is a modern phenomenon; or at least modern consumerism is different from earlier forms. This is not to say that there are no hints of consumerism before the late seventeenth century, in various parts of the world. Several Asian societies had particularly elaborate consumer interests and outlets as part of urban culture. But full-blown consumerism, in terms of intensity, commitment to novelty, and application to numerous social groups, has only been around for 300 years, give or take a few decades.

It is this novelty that makes consumerism so interesting, as part of a historical exploration of how our world came to be as it is.

Consumerism's novelty leads to further assumptions. It is vital to try to explain why consumerism developed and what causes have sustained it. While consumerism may appeal to some "natural" human impulses, it is not purely natural. It requires causes, and part of the larger task of using history to explain what it means involves exploring these causes.

Because consumerism is novel, defying tradition, it also, always, provokes opposition, often deep and durable opposition. Even people who seem to embrace consumerism harbor doubts and guilt. History helps explain these reactions and how they play out even in our own world today.

This is a book about consumerism in world history, and this involves a final set of definable issues. While modern consumerism first arose in the West, everyone knows that by the later nineteenth century it was spreading elsewhere. As already noted, there were vital signs of consumerism in Asia and Africa, before Western forms emerged. But modern consumerism has been wrapped up in issues of Western influence. What is sometimes called "Westernization" involves the spread of consumer behaviors, often under the urgent leadership of European and United States commercial companies. By 2000 Western influence in the world at large rested on consumer standards more than anything else, outlasting military and colonial predominance.

But different societies develop different consumer styles. Even within what is sometimes called the contemporary West, consumerism varies between Western Europe and the United States. The final major analytical issue this book tackles stems from the assumption that, just as consumerism is not simply natural and so must be explained, so it is not always uniform. Hence differences must be identified and explained as well. Differences include different degrees of resistance and different manifestations of hostility and guilt – another topic that remains lively at the outset of the twenty-first century.

Three questions focus the historical exploration of consumerism, beyond illustrating what it is and when and where it emerged. First, why does it happen? Second, how does it change over time, and with what results in terms of the nature of human life and beliefs? And third, how can its manifestations be compared, as consumerism swept across national, cultural and regional boundaries?

And there is a larger evaluative point as well. This book treats consumerism as a neutral development, or at least as a development that mixes advantages and disadvantages, from its origins until the present day. This means that readers are invited to use history to help expand their own assessment of what they find bad and good in consumerism. But it also means that differences in the dates and nature of consumerism must be handled carefully. It is not necessarily "bad" that a society lagged behind the West in consumerism; it is not a sign of some deficiency. Different societies did react to consumerism in terms of prior traditions, and this led to variable outcomes. Indeed, the hold of history in shaping consumerisms is impressive, confirming the utility of a larger historical perspective even on such a pervasive and powerful modern development. But value judgments must be applied with care, in deciding whether Western or Asian or African responses to consumerism are preferable and also which ones require the most elaborate historical explanations. Comparing consumerisms requires flexible understandings, more than an impulse to identify one best way.

All of us know people who "have to have" some item that, objectively, they do not need at all. All of us know people who find emotional solace and personal expression in shopping. Some of us, indeed, are these people. All of us know about societies that seem desperately to want to move to a level of consumerism that will match that of the contemporary United States. Yet all of us know about leaders in many societies who argue against consumerism, who seek to prevent its insidious contagion, and whose resentment of American influence has a great deal to do with concern about consumerist values. This book is about how these types of people and these variations came to be, as fundamental components of the contemporary world.

Acknowledgments

Several people provided invaluable assistance in preparing this book. Jan Cleaver, Veronica Fletcher, and Clio Stearns were able researchers, and Rachel Blanco and Debbie Williams did the final manuscript preparation. Several anonymous readers offered advice on the revised edition, and I benefited greatly from their guidance. Matt Karush offered helpful suggestions for this edition as well. Editors at Routledge have been extremely supportive throughout. I also thank a number of undergraduate and lifelong learning classes at George Mason University for their constructive interest in the subject. A number of people in my personal life have offered useful models of avid consumerism, supplementing my own recurrent passions. This includes a beloved daughter who, at around age five, proclaimed that she was "born to shop" – though she's since calmed down a bit. These friends and relations can accept thanks as well, as they see fit.

Chapter 1

Before modern consumerism

Full-blown consumerism is a modern product. The next chapter will discuss its emergence in Western Europe by the eighteenth century, but before we can usefully discuss its first appearance, we need briefly to discuss its prior absence.

Tackling the nonexistence of a phenomenon in history can get a bit silly. What light on the past, for example, would be shed by a book on the lack of railroads before 1800? Evidence for nonexistence is typically shaky. People do not leave explicit records about their nonparticipation in something they are not aware of.

Yet it is important to sketch how people reacted to material objects, money and shopping before the emergence of modern consumerism, to high-light the change that this emergence involved and, through this, the kinds of causes that combined to bring about major change. This chapter, refer-ring to several different societies before consumerism's full outcropping, offers a baseline by which subsequent developments can be measured. It also suggests a number of traditional alternatives to consumerism – practices that provided meaning and pleasure without being consumerist – that will help explain why, and on what basis, many groups have resisted consumerism in more recent times.

The most obvious non-consumerist feature of traditional, or pre-modern, societies involved widespread poverty: most people did not regularly have enough margin about subsistence to engage in substantial consumerism. But there is more. In most pre-modern societies fairly rigid social hierarchies existed, and upper-class people disapproved of any sign that elements of the lower classes, even if they had a bit of margin, displayed much individual-ism or propensity to cross social boundaries through consumer behaviors. And still more: even in upper classes that did show periodic commitment to con-sumerism, there were recurrent hesitations and counterattacks that limited a consistent consumerist interest. For all classes, other goals – devotion to the public good and/or religion – were meant to override much consumerism. In other words, cultural beliefs, and not just poverty, inhibited consumerism before modern times, and may continue to oppose it even today.

Many of these limitations would continue in modern societies. Poverty, hierarchy, and disapproval hardly disappeared. But in many modern societies their effect was muted because of the rise of consumerist zeal, rather than dominant as in the more traditional antecedents.

Two tricky points

Exploring behavior before consumerism involves two special issues, beyond the general problems of discussing historical nonexistence. Issue one focuses on the upper classes; issue two, less obvious, deals with elements of the masses.

Among many aristocracies and wealthy business minorities, there were strong signs of consumer interests before modern times, in many different societies. For analysts who believe that consumerism is a natural human interest, whenever economic conditions allow, there is real evidence – though there is also evidence that consumerism is an acquired taste, against many basic social impulses.

Two scenarios were particularly common, well before the eighteenth century. Many aristocracies came to delight in fancy luxury products and even novelties, defining their class in part by what can only be called a consumer lifestyle. When merchant groups began to grow in size and wealth, as in China during the Tang dynasty, they too established consumer interests in their urban mansions, sometimes of course trying to imitate the lifestyles of the prestigious aristocracy.

Aristocracies rarely began primarily as consumer classes. Most established themselves through prowess in war and/or special political service. They usually seized a higher-than-usual standard of living in the process, but they hardly qualified as ardent consumers. To take an easy example: many feudal warriors in Europe from the fifth through the twelfth centuries CE, even as they ruled the roost politically and militarily, lived in crude conditions, unadorned by any particular amenities. They might boast a little by way of fancy dress, maybe a few tapestries in their exceptionally drafty mansions or castles. They prized objects such as swords and jewels, sometimes attributing magical power to them (as in the Icelandic *Njal's Saga*, around 1000 CE), which may have some link to consumerism, and they did eat relatively well, particularly in terms of meat consumption. But they were not fully consumer oriented, even though they had resources well above the norm. Into modern times, groups of nobles continued to live in surprisingly crude conditions. This was true, for example, of provincial gentry in Russia in the nineteenth century. Crudeness partly reflected the fact that living standards, while well above peasant levels, were not very high. Earnings were often partly in kind – surplus food from peasant production – rather than in the money needed for consumer purchases. But crudeness also reflected a lack of interest in consumer refinement, even a disdain for soft ways. Consumerism and upper class status were not automatic companions.

Despite this it is also true that, once established and as political conditions settled, many aristocracies did make a fairly explicit transition to a more affluent style of life. Sometimes a debate ensued between defenders of older simplicity, who criticized the frivolousness of new interests and the decline of conventional martial virtue, and the advocates of greater luxury. Rome went through this debate in the later centuries of the Republic. Many aristocrats were consuming luxury products from Greece and the Eastern Mediterranean, developing a passion for silk imported from China, even as critics deplored their debased taste. The critics' arguments focussed on softness, a decline of military zeal and devotion to the public good, not unfamiliar in debates about consumerism even today. Arab warriors went through a similar conversion to more opulent consumer interests by the tenth century, as did the European feudal nobility by the thirteenth century. Again, the common signs were a growing interest in fancy clothing, a taste for key imports (such as sugar, in the case of the European nobles, who developed a pronounced sweet tooth after they encountered sugar during the Crusades), plus a growing interest in decorative objects in the home. And there did come a point when aristocracies, at least the wealthiest segments, identified themselves to each other, and differentiated themselves from other groups, in part on grounds of consumer standards.

Much of what amounted to international trade before modern times focussed on consumer products for the upper classes. People in the Mediterranean cherished Chinese silks. The Roman Empire organized regular trips to India to pick up spices to please aristocratic palates. Arabs used African gold to make jewelry. Many Muslim women sought to accumulate jewelry partly as an investment, to provide financial protection for the future, but also for display and personal expression within the confines of the household. By the postclassical period Chinese porcelain was also widely esteemed. Even Mongol rulers in the fourteenth century delighted in furs that came from African animals.

Obviously, a pre-modern consumerism existed that helped upper classes continue to define themselves, often after an earlier, more militaristic period, and that provided clear pleasure. In this sense the most obvious modern feature of consumerism involves its passage well beyond the upper classes – the motives were not new at all. But by the same token, even where aristocratic consumerism was well developed, the larger society did not embrace consumerism; and even for the upper classes, as we will see, a strong current of disapproval persisted.

The second complexity concerning societies before full consumerism involves arguments based on poverty and subsistence economies. Here, attention shifts from the upper classes to the masses, and particularly that majority of people who in agricultural societies lived as peasants in the countryside.

Before modern times, and if measured by modern standards, most people were poor: often desperately poor. One fundamental reason for the lack of mass consumerism was this poverty. Furthermore, even people above the most desperate levels often lacked much money. Village economies were geared primarily for production for local self-sufficiency. Trade consisted largely of exchanging goods and services within the region, mainly by barter (this was true in colonial New England into the nineteenth century). In these circumstances, not much money circulated, and opportunities to buy consumer items were accordingly constrained.

But here is where the complexity comes in. Peasants were not uniformly poor. Most villages contained a bit of a hierarchy, with some families acquiring more than the average amount of land and definitely maintaining a margin above literal subsistence. Some sold part of their produce on the market – only through this could city populations be sustained – and so also had some money. But they did not primarily use their margin in consumerist ways. Most peasants and urban artisans who were not simply rock bottom poor had non-consumerist values, and this provides the most interesting target for our brief analysis of societies before consumerism. Artisanal guilds, grouping craft workers in cities in Japan, the Middle East, or Western Europe, deliberately discouraged profit maximization and individual display in favor of group solidarity (including standardized craft dress and recreation).

In sum: agricultural societies before modern consumerism characteristically exhibited pronounced inequality. Aristocracies and urban merchant elites often had opportunities for consumer attachments that were unavailable to the masses of ordinary producers. But pronounced hierarchy is not the only complexity involved. Upper classes themselves were not automatically consumerist. More traditional values, often associated with a warrior past, and also religious interests could limit consumerism even when the means were available. From the standpoint of the masses of people, poverty and subsistence-level economic activities were constraints, but here too there were distinctive values involved. Some people had material means beyond survival but simply did not think in consumerist terms. Here, clearly, is a challenge for further exploration.

Dominant value systems

Well before the eighteenth century, various societies around the world had established pervasive value systems, none of which provided a fertile ground for consumerism. Some, indeed, were quite hostile to any potential consumerism, though since widespread consumerism did not exist, the clash was implicit, not explicit.

Several major religions urged their adherents to focus on spiritual, other-worldly goals and argued that worldly goods detracted from the true purposes of earthly life, which should be directed to salvation in a life to come. The scorn for possessions was particularly strong in Buddhism, which had spread widely in southeast and Eastern Asia. Buddhist holy people begged for their subsistence, and a life of contemplation was held up as an ideal. Worldly pleasures were not only meaningless but also dangerous, as they could distract one from spiritual goals. Hinduism had a similar esteem for a life of denial, though there was more accommodation to social groups, such as merchants, that might value some consumerist display. Here too, however, there was no question that the ultimate values were spiritual, not materialistic. Christianity, the dominant religion of Europe and some other areas including parts of the Americas, was also traditionally suspicious of any devotion to material goals. As with Buddhism, the holiest life was a life of poverty; thus in monasteries and convents individuals often divested themselves of possessions. Wealth itself might be suspect, as in Christ's statement that it was easier for a camel to pass through the eye of a needle than for a rich man to gain entry to heaven.

Islam was a bit friendlier to wealth than the other major religions. Merchant activity was compatible with religious goals, and religious leaders approved of profit making, though with certain restrictions. Wealthy people were supposed to give generously to charity for the poor, a fundamental obligation in Islam, and there was no specific discussion of the extent to which remaining earnings might be used for a high standard of living. Finally, as in all the major religions, the real purpose of life was salvation, not enjoyment of material goods. Any attention to wealth that diverted from religious obligations, including regular daily prayer or the pilgrimage to Mecca, was clearly wrong.

Confucianism, the leading belief system of elites in China and some other parts of East Asia, was not a religion at all. It focused on living a good life in society, and, deeply hierarchical, it assumed that the upper class would be wealthy, and appropriately so. But an emphasis on earning wealth, much less spending it in consumerist fashion, was disdained. A gentleman should pay attention to his social obligations and to a life of scholarship, not to blatant spending. Confucian insistence on ritual, including wearing the appropriate costumes, suggested a kind of spending that would not be devoted to novelty or to a joy in acquisition. Ordinary people should not plan on material indulgence at all, for this would contradict appropriate social ranking. Confucian attention to secular rather than religious goals, in other words, created a climate in which consumerism would nevertheless clearly be rejected.

The gap between all the leading religions and secular philosophies and any potential consumerism should not be unduly exaggerated, of course. All the major religions made some peace with wealth, even as they emphasized its threat to holiness. Merchants were a respected caste in Hindu India, and making money was part of being a good merchant. Christian leaders did not systematically attack wealth. By the sixteenth century, the Catholic Church was taking a more sympathetic view of profit making than traditional

Christian leaders. Monks might cheat on vows of poverty, and some monasteries became very wealthy, allowing members to live quite well in material terms. The newer Protestant faith, though firmly committed to the primacy of salvation, actually generated some belief that earning money was a sign of God's favor. (This opening did not include any praise for consumerist display, however.)

Finally, even amid dominant belief systems, individuals might reject or modify approved goals, seeking consumerist joys on their own account. We will see that merchants in many areas, whose activities tested the tolerance both of the leading religions and of Confucianism, often became interested in displaying their success through the acquisition of new goods.

Nevertheless, the tension between leading, well-established value systems and consumerism was important. Upper classes, enjoying a clear margin above subsistence, might be deterred from blatant consumerism by their commitment to religion or Confucianism. Too much display might jeopardize their chance for salvation. In China, using wealth for a life of scholarship might gain more social status than indulgence in the urban high life, given Confucian values. Members of the lower classes, insofar as they were not simply prevented by poverty, might also hesitate about consumerist choices because of their commitment to traditional values.

Furthermore, religion organized some of the impulses that might otherwise seem consumerist (though here, different religions provided different levels of expression; Protestantism, for example, cut back from Catholic levels). Catholic churches were often filled with expensive items – paintings, vestments, even jewelry – designed to glorify God though eye-catching in themselves. Among urban churches some rivalry might develop concerning material display. Mosques stimulated the production of rugs, often breathtaking in design. Even purchases by ordinary people might be justified by spiritual purpose, such as unusually fancy clothing sought for special religious festivals. Interpretation here is tricky. It is easy to argue that purchases for religion could satisfy real consumer interests, but it is equally important to recognize that the interests were not seen as consumerist but rather were devoted to the glory of God.

The disparity between customary value systems and consumerism caused or contributed to three important features in the development of consumerism itself. First, obviously, the disparity helps explain why full consumerism did not exist during most of the long span of world history, even though resources were available above survival level. There is a chicken-and-egg angle here. Did consumerism fail to develop because the value systems inhibited it, or were the value systems partly explainable in terms of the absence of consumerism?

Second, traditional value systems would have to change or reduce their hold before consumerism would become possible. We have already noted shifts in Christianity. By the eighteenth century, more secular value systems rivaled even the newer versions of Christianity in Western Europe, as we will discuss in Chapter 3, thus creating a more favorable cultural context. Changes in Confucianism, Islam, Buddhism, and other religions must be considered in exploring the spread of consumerism worldwide.

But third, the power of traditional value systems, even amid change and reduction in authority, helps explain why opposition and guilt would so often surround consumerism once it did gain ground. Consumerist goals so obviously clashed with Confucian harmony or religious otherworldliness that people, despite embracing consumerism, would often wonder about the validity of their own new interests. Here was the clearest legacy of older beliefs to the brave new world of modern consumerism.

The rich and consumption, before modern consumerism

Modern consumerism does not assume equality, but it does from the first, as we will see, cut across social classes to some degree. Indeed, it can blur class lines, though it never erases the effects of wealth or poverty. When discussing consumption the clearest difference between pre-modern and modern societies is the greater pre-modern gap in spending power and spending habits between rich and poor.

This means, in turn, that we expect to see some consumer display on the part of the small portion of society that was wealthy. Even here, however, there were limits, both in the supply of consumer goods and in the proclivity to indulge in consumerism. This section explores both symptoms and limitations, using examples drawn particularly from China, one of the wealthiest pre-modern societies that also boasted a clear if complicated hierarchical structure.

The issue of pre-modern consumerism does not apply to societies that were not agricultural. Hunting and gathering and nomadic societies simply did not generate a great deal of durable surplus. A few social inequalities might show in the greater decoration or more abundant weaponry available to chiefs and leaders, but there was and could be no commitment to regular acquisition beyond necessities.

Nor were consumerist possibilities particularly extensive in agricultural civilizations before about 800 CE. Wealthy people existed in ancient Athens or Han China. Pericles, in Athens, boasted of the abundance of goods, some brought by trade around the Mediterranean. Wealthy people, in cities and countryside alike, had larger houses with more abundant decoration, and their clothing was more luxurious compared to average standards. Perfume and jewelry were available. By the time of the Roman Empire, if not before, some wealthy people took pleasure in wearing gowns – togas – made from silk imported from China. Rome, in the second century BCE, even featured a brief political debate about consumerism and women. During the bitter wars with Carthage, a law had forbidden women to own more than half an ounce of gold or wear multicolored dresses. With the war over, some male politicians urged that women should have the same rights of display as men, including wearing purple togas; while others argued that wasteful luxury would follow. The law was repealed, partly because the politicians recognized that, with no political rights, women should at least have something to take pride in. Wealth, in other words, brought certain luxuries in classical societies, part of the common distinction between rich minority and poor majority.

Even for the rich, however, there were usually some limits. Trade brought in fancy goods but not a recurrent series of novelties. Luxury existed, in other words, but not the constant parade of changing fashions that would characterize modern consumerism. Furthermore, luxury products themselves were often surprisingly uniform, limiting purely personal expressions. Even Rome's silk togas were standardized, in cut and color, to fit the social category of the aristocratic wearer. There was no sense of using consumption to express great individuality. Luxury existed, but not consumerist fashion.

This situation changed somewhat with advances in upper-class prosperity and in levels of trade in the postclassical period (500–1450 CE). Once the dust settled from the collapse of the great classical empires of Rome, Han China and Gupta India, and as new Afro-Eurasian trade levels developed particularly through the spur of Islamic merchants, aristocrats and some wealthy businessmen had greater opportunity to develop habits that more fully suggested consumerism.

Individual merchants became clear consumerists. In late medieval France, Jacques Coeur built a fancy house in Bourges, filling it with luxury items, some brought back from his travels in the Middle East, and even copying a Middle Eastern bath with running water. A seventeenth-century salt merchant in China, An Lu-tsun, planted orchids all over his home (one of his friends put mechanically controlled nude statues of women in his inner halls, to surprise his guests). An Lu-tsun bought gold foils and watched them drift away from a tower as he released them, and later purchased a series of dolls that he sailed along a local stream. Another competitor designed a huge bronze urinal container for himself, five feet tall, climbing up every night to relieve himself. Merchants of this sort competed with each other in novelties and eccentricities.

There were more general patterns. In China, for example, new luxuries and food and clothing became available to the rich. Previously, drinks such as tea and chocolate had not been available, and even though China produced silk most wealthy people in north China wore coarse hemp cloth. Under the Tang dynasty (618–907) however, things changed. Tea and sugar (this last imported from southeast Asia), and rituals and objects associated with their use, gained great attention among the wealthy. Wu Tzu-mu noted that "the things that people cannot do without every day are firewood, rice, oil, salt, soybean sauce and tea" – a revealing statement in implying that tea, though objectively a consumerist product, had become a necessity. Tea use, and rituals associated with it, spread widely in south China, though northern Chinese remained normally content with boiled water. The Chinese even converted nomadic horsemen to tea use, selling the product to them in return for a supply of war horses – an interesting extension of modest consumerism to a group not usually included. The idea of fashion – clear but also changing standards of dress – appeared at the imperial court as well. One royal consort, Yang Kuei-fei, exerted particular influence through a taste for exotic fads and fancies. Tang fashions spread elsewhere. A tall lady's hat made its way to Europe, where it was called the *hennin* in the French court. Wealthy merchants in China also picked up a taste for fashion, and sections of cities, such as Hang-chou, mixed stores selling novelty items with new kinds of entertainments. Marco Polo described Hang-chou as a pleasure city, with just a bit of over generalization:

> For the people of this city think of nothing else, once they have done the work of their craft and their trade, but to spend a part of the day with their womenfolk, or with hired women, in enjoying themselves either in their barges or in riding about the city in carriages . . . For their minds and thoughts are intent upon nothing but bodily pleasure and the delights of society.

Similar patterns spread from China to Japan. There, by the time of the Tokugawa in the sixteenth century, the imperial court in Kyoto was dominated by protocol, with dress styles governed by strict rules of traditional etiquette, but in more commercial cities, such as Edo, significant attention to changing fashions developed. One historian has even argued that later Japanese success in industrialization was prepared for by its prior experience in dealing with, and manufacturing for, frequent shifts in clothing styles among the wealthy.

Aristocrats in European cities picked up a commitment to fashion as trade accelerated in the later Middle Ages and the Renaissance. St Carlo Borromeo, in sixteenth-century Rome, said that to be a success, one must love God and have a carriage. The revival of classical styles in the Renaissance had a faddish quality, generating interest in shifting novelties.

By the sixteenth century consumer quarters had developed in many cities, not only in China and Europe but also Istanbul, Algiers, and elsewhere. Aristocrats prided and distinguished themselves on the basis of consumer spending, and artisans scurried to provide the necessary goods.

Examples could be multiplied, but the point is clear: wealth generated consumerist interest well before modern times. Cities became known as consumer centers, where trade and profits might concentrate. Still, there are some limits to note, quite apart from the fact that consistent consumerism was possible only to a small minority, even in the wealthiest cities.

Limitation number one: new items were not consistently generated. This meant that some novelties ultimately picked up a traditional tone, no longer creating opportunities for spontaneous new purchases. Tea rituals were a case in point. They required equipment, and for a while this expanded opportunities for creative acquisition. But in time, both in China and in Japan, the equipment became standardized, its purchase a sign of luxury but not really of consumerism. People did not seek the latest craze in teapots and trays; rather, continuity from past styles was the sign of prestige.

More interesting are the periodic attacks on consumerism that dot pre-modern societies – not just moralistic critique, but outright attack in the name of more traditional values. In China, the later Tang dynasty saw one of these counterattacks. Yang Kuei-fei, the striking fashion leader and royal consort, was put to death by disapproving court officials. Whimsical fashion gave way to stricter and less fluctuating rules for dress, even during the otherwise prosperous Song dynasty that followed the Tang. A great deal of attention now went into foot binding as a sign of female beauty, and while this limited women's mobility and made them in a sense consumer objects, it did not encourage consumerism. People began to justify clothing styles, and foot binding itself, purely in terms of tradition. The increasing confinement of women may in itself have limited consumerist interests.

Thus other European observers, entering China in the sixteenth century, described great luxury but no particular sense of fashion. Clothing was chosen according to traditional rules, depending on age, social station, and season of the year. Wealth showed in better quality cloth – linen, silk or satin for the wealthy, cotton for the rest – but not really in style. Only in the choice of carriages did the wealthy Chinese still show a taste for faddish display.

Attacks on consumerism were not confined to China. Many Islamic purists condemned coffee use because it was not mentioned in the Quran. They did not stop the new urban consumer practice, but they did limit it. In Renaissance Europe, religious reformers such as Savanarola periodically emerged to attack luxury and consumption, sponsoring the burning of unnecessary items as part of public purging. Many cities passed sumptuary laws, designed to curb fashion. In the seventeenth century English Puritans were notorious for their hostility to aristocratic fashion, and for a generation they brought it under severe control. None of these movements snuffed out consumer appetite, but they did constrain it. Their periodic success and power suggest the limitations of pre-modern consumerism even among the wealthy: dominant value systems might dispute it successfully.

The result is a mixed one. Signs of consumerism existed before modern times, which is no great surprise. Consumer interest was confined, however, not only to the rich minority but also to certain specific periods. It did not consistently advance. It might be attacked, or it might be constrained by the impulse of the wealthy themselves to prefer traditional styles, that appealed more to propriety and status, over a taste for novelty. Luxury, again, was probably more common than consumerism, even among groups that could afford the latter: that is, displays of wealth but along fairly standardized patterns, without rapid fashion shifts or opportunities for individuality. This is why, in addition to the limited numbers of the wealthy, no consistent consumerist industries arose before modern times.

Limits on pre-modern consumerism, beyond sheer poverty, thus include: the tendency to prefer standard displays, which often designated membership in a group, over a stylishness defined in terms of novelty; recurrent, sometimes brutal, attacks on consumerism itself; and the larger devotion, if not of every individual at least of society as a whole, to religious and collective goals.

Ordinary people

As we have seen, the most obvious point about consumerism and the masses of people, peasants particularly but also urban artisans and laborers, is that few had enough economic margin above subsistence, particularly in terms of money earnings, to indulge in anything like consumerism. An occasional trinket might attract the eye, but there was no regular basis for commitment.

This fact was reflected in common trading patterns, particularly in the countryside where most people lived. Opportunities for shopping were limited. An occasional peddler passed through, and this might be an opportunity for mild indulgence. Some rural people traveled to town periodically for a commercial fair or market. These open-air markets mainly exchanged food items and some clothing or tools, but an occasional acquisition beyond necessities might be possible. Most peasants produced almost everything for themselves, from food to clothing to homes themselves, and this was not a system in which consumerism could take root.

The most regularly purchased item throughout most agricultural civilizations was salt, which is why salt merchants, as for example in China, could make so much money. Salt was used primarily to preserve meat. On occasion, as in China under the Tang and also in Arab Islam, salt purchases expanded greatly, which suggests improvements in prosperity that allowed people to consume more meat rather than relying on a purely vegetable diet. This is an interesting and important development, but it hardly suggests consumerism. Trade, quite simply, neither reflected nor encouraged mass consumerism.

But there is more involved here than the undeniable material limitations of ordinary existence. As with the aristocracy and urban elite, distinctive goals constrained consumerism. Many people, who did produce or could produce a bit more than they or their families needed to subsist, simply did not think in consumerist terms. There are several related points here in addition to the absence of many faddish goods or sales outlets.

First, many peasants clearly valued acquiring more land, when resources permitted, over any other material goal. Their concern was security, for themselves and for future generations, not a subsequent basis for more varied consumption. Peasant land hunger would war with potential consumerism in Western Europe until after World War II.

Second, many peasants and urban workers found it perfectly logical and desirable to contribute part of their surplus to community works, some of which might well displace potential individual consumer goals. European towns and villages vied with each other, for example, over who could build the tallest church steeple or have the biggest bell. Modern consumerism does not entirely replace public spending with private goals, but it offers a different balance. The sense of participation in a community, with spending directed toward collective, and often religious, goals, ran stronger in the pre-consumerist world.

Finally, many peasants and artisans worried that too much display of consumer success would be inappropriate in terms of group and sometimes religious norms. Peasant culture in most parts of the world did not insist on equality, but it did frown on too much individualism. The same held true for craft guilds, which from Europe to Japan worked hard to make sure no single producer earned too much more than his colleagues or demonstrated a particularly affluent style of life. Group norms also directed much of the spending that did occur, for families with a small economic margin above subsistence. Village festivals were collective occasions, with colorful costumes determined by tradition (at least in principle) rather than individual, consumerist choice. The same held true of artisan guilds, with their standardized uniforms and emblems for public display on special occasions. Both villages and guilds also encouraged community feasts, another key use of surplus on the many festival occasions that dotted the traditional calendar. These expressions could provide real satisfaction, even a participation in beauty and fantasy, but they were not consumerist expressions and easily preempted the emergence of such expressions in pre-modern societies. People did not shop for faddish new items to wear to the next festival: they did not seek to single themselves out as individuals. Festivals emphasized group solidarity and repetition – the same styles and entertainments year after year, providing genuine pleasure but in a way that differed from modern consumerism.

Ordinary people, then, even more than the wealthy, were part of cultures that did not operate in a consumerist direction, and extensive poverty was not the sole reason for this. Beliefs, the gap between rich and poor, the organization of manufacturing and trade all combined not to block consumerism – because this would imply an option that simply did not exist – but to provide alternative meanings, alternative definitions of the results of economic endeavor.

Conclusion

Even the interests and behaviors of the wealthy would have to change some-what before a consumer society could emerge. Indulgence in innovation would have to gain ground over reliance on set forms of costume and decoration. Ordinary people would have to change even more. Established beliefs – in otherwordly religious goals, but also in the importance of maintaining hierarchy and group insignia and the pleasure derived from repetition of styles as opposed to innovation – long would work against consumerism. Societies everywhere had built meaningful behaviors that served as alternatives to consumerism; they were not just impoverished, waiting around for the prosperity that would allow them to exercise some natural human propensity to consume. The very existence of cherished traditions would offer a further barrier to consumerism, which would often be criticized for its novelty (and for its foreignness), for its variance from established ways.

This is why, as we will note in the next chapter, something of a revolution had to occur before consumerism emerged. But change was possible, and a revolution, all the more striking because such well-established patterns had operated successfully for so long, did take shape in many different specific settings.

Several other conclusions emerge from a consideration of societies before full consumerism. First, consumerism was impeded by a combination of strong social divisions, widespread poverty, and alternative values. But second, signs of consumer interest abounded. Even the laws and religious rules that sought to limit consumer indulgence demonstrated that there were powerful impulses in play. Whether it is best to view some societies as consumerist, but simply lacking the full apparatus of modern consumerism, or as in this chapter, not really consumerist, can be debated. The debate, however, might become sterile, for either approach can accommodate the two main points, that is, an absence of modern-style consumerism but the existence of consumer behavior among some groups at some times.

There is a third point. Some societies went farther toward early forms of consumerism than others. Areas that placed particular emphasis on colorful dress and appearance, as in many parts of sub-Saharan Africa, were different from societies that constrained self-presentations. China, despite counter-currents, clearly went relatively far toward consumerism in comparison with some other societies. Differences of this sort would have an impact later on, after the conditions for modern consumerism emerged. The precise patterns of modern consumerism would reflect earlier customs, even as new ingredients were added.

We have also noted some change over time. Each major period of world history generated larger cities, in the most prosperous societies, and higher levels of international trade. Opportunities for consumerism increased apace, particularly for the upper classes but sometimes lower down the social scale.

China, self-sufficient in most items, depended on trade in southeast Asia for tea and certain spices by the postclassical period. Then, after 1500, it began to import increasing amounts of silver, partly to bolster its money system – the government would ultimately require that taxes be paid in silver, rather than paper money – but also partly for jewelry and adornment. Many urban people began to display a growing prosperity. It was also after 1500 that coffee (imported from Africa) and coffee houses began to spread in the Middle East, despite widespread official disapproval. Previously used for religious purposes, coffee now became a standard consumer item, around which men (with women largely excluded) began to organize intense social activities. Soon, coffee would spread to Europe, with similar effects (and also similar criticisms, by officials who thought in terms of devotion to traditional goods rather than novelties). The use of sugar began to expand in Europe as well, again reaching below the levels of the very wealthy. International trade was heating up, and so were new opportunities for consumerism. Here, clearly, was a context for further change.

Further reading

For a challenging guide to pre-modern consumerism but also its limitations: S.A.M. Adshead, *Material Culture in Europe and China, 1400–1800* (New York: St Martin's Press, 1997). See also William T. Rowe, *Hankow: Commerce and Society in a Chinese City, 1796–1889* (Stanford, CA: Stanford University Press, 1984). On China's vibrant commercial economy and its influence: André Gunder Frank, *Reorient: Global Economy in the Asian Age* (Berkeley: University of California Press, 1998) and Kenneth Pomeranz and Steven Topik, *The World that Trade Created: Society, Culture, and the Economy, 1400 to the Present* (Armonk, NY: M.E. Sharpe, 1999). On the rise of coffee as a new consumer interest: Stewart Allen, *The Devil's Cup: Coffee, the Driving Force in History* (New York: Soho, 1999).

Part I

The emergence of consumerism in the West

Chapters in this section deal with the origins of modern consumer society in Western Europe and with its relatively quick spread to the United States. The time frame involves, first, the seventeenth and particularly eighteenth centuries, when the first manifestations occurred, but then the nineteenth and early twentieth centuries when change picked up momentum and when stronger countercurrents emerged. The key historical themes involve change, some comparison, and an understanding of a certain amount of complexity. The issues are challenging, but fairly straightforward: what was new about consumerism? What caused it, and how have historians discussed causation? Why did people in the United States respond relatively quickly to consumerist impulses (but also: why did they initially lag behind countries such as England and France)? Finally, in all its initial sites, consumerism showed some standard features but also some differentiations according to social group and gender. It also featured tensions between comfort and a desire to impress by means of display (often by accepting uncomfortable styles). These are some of the complexities that must be handled in any interpretation of what consumerism involved.

Once launched, consumerism had the potential to develop further. Chapter 5 deals with the subsequent development of consumerism in the later nineteenth and early twentieth centuries. Here the leading questions are: what changed, as opposed simply to extending initial directions, and what were the additional causes involved? Finally, rounding out the analysis of Western consumerism, Chapter 6 takes up the criticism and private guilts that consumerism provoked, both initially and into the twentieth century. These hesitations can subsequently be compared with reactions in other parts of the world, where consumerism would be not only new but partly foreign.

Overall, the chapters in this section cover more than two centuries, between the first full emergence of modern consumerism in the early eighteenth century and its wider consolidation by the 1920s in the Western world. This period may be surprisingly short, given the amount of innovation involved. And of course there were still further changes to come, as consumerism has continued to evolve in Europe and the United States.

But before picking up the most recent extensions in Chapter 11, Part II will turn to consumerism on a world scale, which began to take shape in the 1850s but under somewhat different circumstances from ongoing developments in the West.

Chapter 2

The emergence of consumerism

The discovery of significant consumerism, of the modern sort, in eighteenth-century Western Europe was a major historical find. It has significantly reshaped the way we think about modern social history and about consumerism itself – particularly its causes and initial meanings. This chapter lays out what initial consumerism was, in terms both of apparatus – the new sales techniques, outlets and goods – and in terms of human behavior and perceived needs. The first part, of course, is more measurable than the second.

Historians love to dispute about origins. Because strong traces of consumer interest and behavior go well back in human history, as we have seen, it is not surprising that some components of European consumerism predate the eighteenth century. There was something of a gradual buildup within the larger global context of accelerating international trade and urbanism. And it may be that, ultimately, it will be the later seventeenth rather than the eighteenth century that will hold pride of place for the fuller emergence of consumerism. Whatever the precise boundary line between preparatory steps and flowering, it is clear that a consumer society existed by the mid-eighteenth century in Britain, France, the Low Countries, and parts of Germany and Italy. Some traces also have spilled over into the British colonies in North America, though this will be taken up in a later chapter. Not surprisingly, consumerism first centered in the regions where a commercial economy was most fully developed and where access to global products was expanding most rapidly.

Initial signs of consumerism include the growing market for sugar. Wealthy people in Europe had indulged a taste for sugar since the late Middle Ages. This prompted further development of sugar production in new European colonies, first in the islands of the southern Atlantic, such as the Azores, then in the Americas. This production, in turn, spurred a larger market, making sugar, in the terms of one anthropologist, the world's first mass consumer good. Sugar purchases did not constitute full consumerism, but they did suggest a new taste for indulgence in a food that was by no means necessary. Other kinds of purchases drew attention also. Spending on household furnishings increased for people above the poverty line, as early as the sixteenth century. Better beds, with cloth rather than straw mattresses, were one item. Decorated cabinets provided work for hosts of nameless craftsmen, even in the countryside.

Tulips were another novelty purchase, reaching many people in the seventeenth century. Initially imported from Asia in the sixteenth century, tulip purchases became a genuine passion by the 1630s, particularly of course in Holland. New varieties were developed – another consumerist symptom – and by the 1640s speculators were trading on future tulip consumption. Paintings of tulips and other flowers were a related consumer item. While the tulip craze hinted at consumerism, it was not widely available to ordinary people; and when the craze passed, it was not immediately followed up by another fad, as would become standard when consumerism was fully installed.

Expansion of colonial trade and profit spurred an escalation of consumer purchases toward the end of the seventeenth century. This was when consuming tea and coffee began to be fashionable. Coffee houses would become a staple public venue in eighteenth-century cities, but the new items were also consumed in the home. This in turn prompted growing interest in fancier serving sets, including coffee- and teapots. For the wealthy, these might be sought in porcelain imported from China – material that in fact began to be called china, in the seventeenth century – but a market developed below this level as well. Imports also played a vital role in clothing. Cotton fabrics from India drew wide attention, because they could be dyed in bright colors and because they were cheap and easily washable. Here too was a field soon exploited by European producers.

The consumer apparatus

The most easily measured aspect of eighteenth-century consumerism consisted of an explosion of shops and new marketing methods, and the change was dramatic indeed. Older types of exchange, with peddlers and fairs, continued as well, and in some cases expanded in bringing hints of consumer goods to remote areas. But it was the shopkeeper and his methods that anchored the first iteration of a consumer society.

Indeed, what one group of historians has called the consumer revolution was based on the realization by shopkeepers and consumer goods producers that wants and needs were infinitely stretchable, not confined to what was required to live up to conventional standards or to subsist. Imaginative storeowners began to pull out all the stops to lure customers. They set up enticing window displays. They featured bargain items, even selling at a loss to get customers into the store – where they might buy more expensive goods. (This practice of using "loss leaders" obviously continues today.) A comment in 1747 noted; "A custom has prevailed among Grocers to sell Sugars for the Prime Cost, and they are out of Pocket by the Sale;" but purchases of "other Commodities" for which customers paid "extravagant prices" made up for the loss. Consumer credit was widely extended, again, to help people buy what they did not need. Leading outlets gave gifts to notables, hoping that their example would inspire others to "have to have" the same item.

Relatively humble shopkeepers invented special gimmicks. One such, in England, named Martin von Butchell, a former dentist who sold medicine, highlighted his own eccentricities. He rode a "white pony which he sometimes painted all purple and sometimes with spots," to advertise himself and through this his wares. A picture from 1747 shows another salesman dressed like a high fashion lady, to draw attention to the gingerbread he was selling.

Use of advertisements proliferated. They filled the weekly newspapers now available in the cities. They contributed to posters and trade cards that were widely distributed. Fashion magazines with drawings first developed in France in the 1670s, but England developed the genre still further. Fashion prints became common by the 1770s. Advertisers began to insert pictures of the latest hats and dresses into pocket books and almanacs, specifically designed for "ordinary young gentlewomen, not the extravagant few." Fashion dolls, often imported from France, were also used to stimulate taste. Most advertisements, however, consisted of words, not visuals, given the available print technology. Newspapers featured paragraph-length ads, looking like news inserted in news columns. Vivid claims made up for the limitations of the medium. The *London Morning Post*, in 1783, thus described a new bed:

> In the celestial bed no feather is employed . . . springy hair mattresses are used . . . in order that I might have for the important purposes, the strongest and most springy hair, I procured at vast expense, the tails of English stallions, which when twisted, baked and then untwisted and properly prepared, is elastic to the highest degree.
>
> But the chief elastic principle of my celestial bed is produced by artificial lodestones. About fifteen hundred pounds' weight of artificial and compound magnets are so disposed and arranged as to be continually pouring forth in an ever-flowing circle inconceivably and irresistibly powerful tides of magnetic effluxion, which is well known to have a very strong affinity with the electric fire . . . fully impregnated moreover, with the balmly vivifying effluvia of restorative balsamic medicines . . . It is impossible, in the nature of things, but that strong, beautiful, brilliant, nay double-distilled children . . . must infallibly be begotten.

Here, obviously, huge claims, backed by invocations of science, suggested the full power of the advertising imagination. In case the message was lost, that the bed would produce higher-quality children, the biblical message

"Be fruitful, multiply and replenish the earth" was imprinted, in "burnished" gold, on the head of the bed.

Advertisers also used testimonials from the rich and famous. A razor-strop manufacturer named Packwood claimed that noblemen wrote to him to praise his product – "that ease, with which my beard was taken away, entirely resulted from the virtue of PACKWOOD's newly-invented Strops." Public opinion was also invoked for this fashionably novel product:

> Public opinion on the power of Packwood's superior Razor Strop agree that it is worth its weight in gold, and acknowledge their face to be cleaner in the evening (by the use of the Strop) than it used to be immediately after shaving in the morning.

Packwood also placed his ads in merchant newspapers, destined for traders and ships' officers in the East India area, noting that his items took up little space but, again, "are acknowledged to be worth their weight in gold."

Finally, manufacturers began to combine with shopkeepers to stimulate but also to check on public taste. Josiah Wedgwood, the pottery maker known also for his innovations in the production process, begged his sales force to keep him informed of any new whim. We can "make you new Vases like lightning when you think we may do it with safety," he wrote at one point, asking whether the public was ready for a new "Grecian" style. New designs were tested in selected outlets before being mass-produced, while regular reports also warned that tastes were shifting and that production of some of the older lines should be halted. Wedgwood again: "It is always of the first consequence to us to know what does not, as well as what does sell." Production and sales now consisted of a combination of trying to whip up enthusiasm for a new craze, with studying how tastes were spontaneously shifting. The goal was to be able to change frequently, so that people who had bought one set of plates or vases would have to come back again lest their possessions be out of date.

The apparatus of the consumer revolution involved inventing or embellishing virtually every sales technique that consumerism still employs. The technology was different from that of our own time, quite obviously. Reaching individual homes was more difficult, use of visual imagery more restricted. But the grandiose themes of advertising were already fully established, as were the methods of drawing people into stores, lending money for items not really required, and adjusting production lines to fashion whims.

What they bought

The goods involved in the first consumer revolution were varied. Most, understandably enough, shaded off from necessity, though there were a few breakthroughs toward really new consumer items.

Clothing headed the list. Early in the eighteenth century tall hats, wigs, and wide skirts became the rage for women. In 1711 the critic Addison wrote ironically of "the ladies" that "the whole sex is now dwarfed and shrunk into a race of beauties that seems quite another species" because of their massive attire. People began to refer to an "epidemical madness" to consume the latest fashions; they talked of "universal" contagions and "infections," referring to the compulsive power of clothing styles. Printed cotton cloth became a key craze. So did new undergarments, including stays and corsets designed to mold the body. Monthly fashion shows in cities such as London and Paris set the tone, but local salesmen could advertise that they had "just returned from Town with the newest Fashions," with equal effect. Provincial newspapers carried regular reports on styles in cities such as London or Paris. One British observer noted that, in one town, "the wives and daughters of the most topping tradesmen vie with each other every Sunday in the elegance of their apparel."

The ripple effect of consumerism drew quick comment, for the styles of the higher classes could easily be imitated in cheaper models designed for wider sale. One sour critic noted:

> It is the curse of this nation that the laborer and the mechanic will ape the lord, the different ranks of people are too much confounded: the lower orders press so hard on the heels of the higher, if some remedy is not used the Lord will be in danger of becoming the valet of his Gentleman.

"The different stations of Life so run into and mix with each other, that it is hard to say, where the one ends, and the other begins." Domestic servants were particularly noted for imitating the styles of the ladies they served. "A fondness for Dress may be said to be the folly of the age, and it is to be lamented that it has nearly destroyed those becoming marks whereby the several classes of society were formerly distinguished."

Clothing interests could extend to other items of apparel. A passion for watches spread widely in the eighteenth century, particularly for men. Historians used to note the rapid spread of clocks and watches as a sign that people were becoming increasingly conscious of clock time, and this is to some extent accurate. But many people initially bought watches in order to look up-to-date, to be the first in their group to have one. Only later would they learn actually to tell time and use the item.

Items to beautify the body in other ways won attention. We have already noted the enthusiasm claimed for new shaving devices for men. Perfume sales began to mushroom. People, particularly in the middle and upper classes, began to become more conscious of "bad" smells from the late eighteenth century onward: masking the body was a durably important response, and a goldmine for certain products.

In addition to clothing, household items constituted the second major line of consumerism. Here too, as with Wedgwood's china, new styles and tastes could be endlessly invented. The eighteenth century would see a proliferation of Greek styles, rivaling Gothic motifs, along with genuinely new designs. Wills reveal a steady expansion of furnishings plus brass, pewter, and china items, by the later seventeenth and the eighteenth centuries, even in relatively ordinary households. Beds had improved earlier and still commanded attention, but the percentage outlays for bedding actually declined as other objects, headed by tableware, gained greater attention. Glassware, china, knives and forks, tea equipment, and table cloths increasingly became necessities, reflecting serious changes in the rhythms as well as the physical context for family life. In 1711 an English magazine urged all "well-regulated families" to take an hour each morning for breakfast at home, of course with the proper "Tea Equipage."

Quite simply, by the eighteenth century, people were investing more of their incomes into consumer goods. Home furnishing items pioneered by the upper classes, particularly in the cities, progressively fanned out to more urban lower-class homes and to the countryside, throughout the Atlantic world.

And consumerism could extend into other areas. Items explicitly designed for children constituted one new area. Toy manufacturing began, with some of the same market testing as with items for the home. Books explicitly designed for children constituted another new consumer item. Older fairy stories were adapted for a child audience for the first time, and eager entrepreneurs also commissioned new books. Children did not yet constitute a direct consumer market; purchasing was done by parents, mostly middle-class, eager to buy items that would educate and improve their offspring. Promotions for the books set the tone: "A Play-book for children to allure them to read as soon as possible" – "to decoy children into reading."

While a fully consumerist leisure did not yet exist, there were important developments. Circuses were organized for the first time in Europe, starting in France in the late seventeenth century. Attractions were set up to teach children science through exhibits of curiosities, with family tickets advertised. Coffeehouses of course offered not only coffee, but also reading matter for adults – another contact with consumerism. It was also in the late eighteenth century that restaurants began to open (as opposed to inns designed to feed travelers), where people would go to buy meals to please their taste. The idea of fine foods, or what the French (who led in this development) called gastronomy was closely attached to this aspect of consumerism.

By the eighteenth century, in fact, the list of items that people regarded as necessities was beginning to expand, a key facet of consumerist development. During the French Revolution, for example, Parisian workers insisted that they be provided with "goods of prime necessity." by which they meant sugar, soap, candles, and coffee. The list included three things (candles were the exception) that would have seemed clear luxuries just a century before. (But just before the Revolution, Parisians had been consuming two and a half million pounds of coffee and six and a half million pounds of sugar per year.) And other products were coming close to being necessities. Pipe tobacco was one, a clearly masculine item. Cosmetics, including not only perfume but also rouge, were in wide use, as were decorative buttons and other kinds of cheap jewelry. The French Revolution also generated its own consumer items, in the form of new medals, new clothing fashions, and special hats.

Consumerist needs

Describing the apparatus and goods of consumerism already raises questions about the functions, the human needs that new levels of consumption were serving. When new products moved from novelty to necessity, when observers talked of people obsessed with fashionable clothing, something more than adroit salesmanship was involved. Acquiring goods was becoming part of individuals' identity, their measurement of what a satisfactory life involved.

Two particular aspects of the consumer revolution drive this point home. The first was theft. The same raging compulsions that drove some people to thirst for the latest style drove others, unable to indulge their needs, to steal. Second-hand trade in dresses, shoes, ribbons, and scarves brought the price down, but this was not necessarily enough. The rate of theft of clothing rose rapidly in the eighteenth century, with men and women both involved. Shops were not the only targets. Penelope Coleman stole a pair of gold earrings, and pair of stays and a calico apron from Sarah Garshier, a young girl inexperienced in adult wiles. Some people, women as well as men, stripped people naked by violence or threat. (Drunks were a common target.) Servants stole clothing from their mistresses and masters, travelers from fellow-lodgers at inns. Friends stole from each other, when they visited at home. The need for stylish or novel items might easily overcome normal restraint. Not surprisingly, people also went deep into debt to cover consumer goods they thought they needed. Thus a new artisan apprentice in London, from a farming family, detailed the shoes, jacket, socks, ruffled shirt, and hat he sported, while going heavily into debt.

On the other side of the law, people began to name consumer items lovingly in their wills, hoping to pass down a cherished piece of furniture or dress as an emblem of affection. Material objects, here, focussed and symbolized emotion. Women, particularly, even from relatively modest households, went into their possessions in great detail when making out wills. They listed clothing, furnishings, tableware, jewelry, clocks, and books. One woman left her "best long scarf" to a cherished friend, again because of the personal meaning the item had. Household items were passed on, one by one, to members of families. Mirrors, china tea sets, and silver items of various sorts, from candlesticks to shoe buttons, came in for special attention. Here, the role of consumer goods in family life could persist after death, with the goods distributed to individuals who had particularly fancied them as a sign of affection.

New ideas of comfort accompanied other meanings of consumer goods. People began to comment on older homes in terms of how uncomfortable they were. They began to dislike smells that had previously passed without notice, claiming among other things that they kept them awake. A number of new inventions, including the Franklin stove, were designed to reduce smokiness within the home, as part of the new quest for comfort. This new attention to comfort was part of redefining items that had once seemed luxuries into necessities, as with certain types of home furnishings or the availability of tea on a cold day. Clothing was also now rated in terms of comfort. Changes of clothing were now seen as desirable, and good for the health (again, washable cottons were a godsend here). A London doctor related comfort to expanding consumerism directly:

> The Wants of the Mind are Infinite, Man naturally Aspires, and as his Mind is elevated, his Senses grow more refined, and more capable of Delight; his Desires are enlarged (*sic*) and his Wants increase with his Wishes, which is for everything that is rare, can gratify his Senses, adorn his Body, and promote the Ease, Pleasure and Pomp of Life.

A growing interest in umbrellas provides a fascinating example of the consumerist standards of comfort, and how new they were. People began to dislike getting wet, something that seemingly had never greatly bothered them before. Apparently borrowed from Chinese example, umbrellas were introduced to Parisian nobility in the seventeenth century, and then began to move down the social scale. In rainy England, umbrellas passed into wide use from the 1770s onward. They were criticized as being foreign and effete: Horace Walpole, an essayist, blasted the French for "walking about the streets in the rain with umbrellas to avoid putting on their hats." But the invasion of umbrellas could not be stopped, and soon began to be associated with Englishness.

Comfort did not always prevail. Most furniture was valued more for gentility than comfort, and chairs, particularly, were stiff and unyielding. Other items were debatable. Some people contended that corsets and stays, for women, improved comfort by artificially supporting the body, but there were critics who contended that fashion forced women to fit into unpleasant contortions. Consumerism could be complex.

Finally, consumerism gains additional meaning through the advent of the idea of boredom, another eighteenth-century innovation. Surely people had been bored before consumerism, but in English, at least, they had no word to describe their condition. Now they did. In a society increasingly impressed by novelty and acquisition, it became easier to deplore a lack of interest and stimulation – to note, in sum, that one was bored. Novelists began to write frequently of boredom (for which consumerism might be a cure). Here is another indication of the profound changes in human perception that consumerism involved.

Conclusion

The arrival of consumerism in Western Europe involved truly revolutionary change in the ways goods were sold, in the array of goods available and cherished, and in the goals people defined for their daily lives. This last, of course – the redefinition of needs and aspirations – is the core feature of consumerism, though also the hardest to define. Questions remain. We do not yet know how many people were involved in what levels of consumerism. Some items were still largely reserved for the wealthy. Urbanites clearly had more opportunities than rural people (still the vast majority). Yet consumerism did have more democratic aspects, as witness the spread of household items, the claims of French revolutionaries, the signs of change in the countryside or the prevalence of theft. The problem is knowing how many people really could join the full consumerist parade, or even wanted to.

The depth of commitment of those involved is also hard to fathom. Some people, clearly, and not just the wealthy, took issues of stylishness and comfort very seriously indeed. But others may have dabbled, perhaps particularly in their youth, without committing themselves deeply to a lifetime of keeping up with every new whim. These issues continue to complicate an assessment of consumerism even today, but they are particularly challenging in the initial period. Many people were poor; many were illiterate; many had little contact with trendsetters of any variety. The consumer revolution was very real, but it did not, immediately, establish the range or level of participation that would develop later on.

It is also important to remember objections and countervailing forces. Even as consumerism gained ground in the eighteenth century, other currents pointed in different directions. The Methodist religion spread in Britain and its North American colonies, for example, emphasizing obedience to God and downplaying materialism. More broadly, what some historians have called a "Protestant ethic" spread among various groups, urging hard work but also self-denial and saving, rather than consumption. These movements did not prevent consumerism – some individuals might believe in the Protestant ethic but still demonstrate some of their success through consumerism – but they do suggest complexity. Explicit objections to consumerism also developed. Many critics blasted the frivolity of the lower classes or of women, basically arguing that established hierarchies should be protected against consumerism. King Frederick the Great of Prussia condemned popular coffee drinking, arguing that beer should be good enough for his subjects; here, simple traditionalism plus a reaction against foreign products motivated concern. We have seen that even comfort drew its opponents, eager to see traditional hardiness enshrined.

By the same token, of course, the chorus of objections to consumerism, while important, also demonstrates both the prevalence and the novelty of the new interests. If consumerism had been a minor eruption, or if it simply expressed a set of natural cravings, it would have passed without notice. People at the time had some sense of change, and today in hindsight we can see even more clearly: a significant reorientation was underway.

The revolution that did occur obviously must be explained. Why did many people generate new and passionate attachments to things? Assessing the causes of the new consumerism is a clear challenge to historical analysis. For without grasping the causes, the whole phenomenon loses meaning. People do not redefine what life is about very frequently; some powerful forces must have been involved.

Further reading

John Brewer and Roy Porters, eds, *Consumption and the World of Goods* (New York: Routledge, 1993); Elizabeth Kowaleski-Wallace, *Consuming Subjects: Women, Shopping and Business in the Eighteenth Century* (New York: Columbia University Press, 1997); Maxine Berg and Helen Clifford, eds, *Consumers and Luxury: Consumer Culture in Europe 1650–1850* (Manchester: Manchester University Press, 1999); Lorna Weatherill, *Consumer Behavior and Material Culture in Britain, 1660–1760* (New York: Routledge, 1988); Neil McKenrick, Colin Brewer, and J.A. Plumb, *The Birth of a Consumer Society: The Commercialization of Eighteenth-Century England* (Bloomington: Indiana University Press, 1982) – a pioneering study; Carole Shammas, *The Pre-Industrial Consumer in England and America* (Oxford: Clarendon, 1990). On women and early consumerism: G.J. Barker Benfield, *Culture of Sensibility: Sex and Society in Eighteenth-Century Britain* (Chicago: University of Chicago Press, 1992).

Chapter 3

The first causes of consumerism

The rise of consumerism in eighteenth-century Western Europe involved an array of new goals and behaviors. In addition to the novel methods of the shopkeepers and producers, hosts of individual people were reevaluating what the goals in life should be, and what brought happiness. A change of this magnitude inevitably raises questions about causation. Given the absence of extensive consumerism before this point, some serious combination of factors was essential to turn commercial systems and, above all, personal motivations in new directions.

Exploring causes is interesting in its own right, involving some real detective work. It helps relate change to other developments in European history at that point. And it adds to our understanding of what consumerism itself meant, what needs it served in personal and social life. Yet figuring out causation is also demanding. Unlike laboratory scientists, historians cannot exactly reproduce past phenomena in order to test variables. In the case of consumerism, particularly, there remains a great deal of debate – because the initial rise of consumerism itself was discovered only recently. Not surprisingly, several factors were involved, as is usually the case with a change in behavior of this magnitude.

One way to break down the debate is to divide causes between the reasonably obvious – factors that clearly helped generate consumerism, but did not necessarily provide the clearest or fullest spark – and factors that may explain more but that are a bit more diffuse.

No one, as consumerism first developed, sat down to write an essay on why consumer needs were gaining ground. Consumerism in this sense contrasts with past events such as wars, where some people do discuss motivations at the time. The phenomenon was noticed by critics, who deplored what they saw as false goals, but it was often attributed to conventional vices such as greed that may well have been in play but do not really help to explain change because they are not new. Historians are on their own in explaining the first stages of this huge modern development. Their ongoing debate remains inconclusive, but it is also enlightening.

Specific factors and preconditions

Some people might try to explain consumerism very simply, as follows. The desire to acquire new goods is part of human nature: all that must be added, historically, is greater prosperity, a margin of money earnings above subsistence, so that the delight in acquisition can be indulged. Give a person more money than he absolutely needs, and he'll become a consumerist.

In terms of causes, this explanation is wrong, or at least oversimplified. We have seen that many people in the past, who did have a margin over subsistence, did not behave like systematic consumerists. This point would reemerge in Western Europe in the early nineteenth century, as we will discuss later in this chapter. Human nature rarely explains a change tied to a particular point in time, like modern consumerism.

It is true, however, that an increase in prosperity was vital to consumerism's advent. The European economy began to become more commercial from the sixteenth century onward. European dominance of international trade, including the slave trade, brought new levels of profit to many merchants, and some of this spread among peasants and manufacturing workers who produced for the market. More people began growing or manufacturing goods for sale, rather than for local subsistence. Trade and specialization advanced individual prosperity and access to money. The development was not universal. There was also a growing group of people dependent on wage labor, who often suffered rather than prospered. New problems of poverty were noted along with growing wealth, a combination that often continues in commercial economies. This means that Western society was long divided between people who could afford new consumer indulgences, and a large number enmeshed in poverty, or so worried about their chances of falling into poverty that they would rigorously limit consumer activity.

As early as the sixteenth century, though, some observers began to note new uses of wealth among relatively ordinary people, both rural and urban. The quality of bedding and other furnishings improved for some. More houses sported glass windows. Here were hints both of growing money earnings and of early consumerist uses, in countries such as England. More money earnings did not, it must be repeated, guarantee consumerism, and full consumer behaviors did not immediately emerge. But higher earnings were a vital precondition, and they surely did play on "human nature" to some extent. New forms of money earnings are always involved in the rise of consumerism, around the world.

Add to new earnings, and some human nature impulses, the factors of new goods and new marketing procedures, and some interpreters might argue that the explanation is complete. Increasing European involvement in world trade, and the rise of colonial production, undoubtedly brought attractive new goods to the attention of masses of consumers. Sugar, as the historical anthropologist has noted, was the first mass consumer good, deliberately produced and imported for people to buy with money (since it was not locally grown, it could not be part of regional exchange arrangements). On its heels came coffee and tea. Here were direct new stimuli to consumer tastes, and around them developed other consumer items such as serving utensils, including the ubiquitous teapot. Cotton cloth soon followed, initially imported from India and then produced in Europe directly.

Then came the new swarms of shopkeepers and their enticing methods, discussed in the previous chapter. With eye-catching window displays, news-paper advertisements, loss leaders, and other gimmicks, no wonder people began to think they had new needs. Explicit studies of consumer tastes, such as those pioneered by Wedgwood for porcelain, added to the mix.

One causation approach, then, might simply be this: important elements of human nature are open to delight in the acquisition of new goods. Add growing prosperity and money earnings, which allowed these elements to shine through. Add attractive new goods and marketing methods that provided new opportunities to manipulate ordinary folks and build on their natural impulses and their new earnings. And the result is assured: consumerism will emerge and grow.

Historians dealing with eighteenth-century Western Europe often insist on one final standard component: the desire to emulate the upper classes, and particularly the aristocracy. Europe was unquestionably a highly strati-fied society. The aristocracy, equally unquestionably, displayed consumer interests. During the seventeenth century, for example, in venues such as the great court at Versailles, aristocrats had tried to outdo each other with fancy costumes (both male and female), luxurious coaches, and elegant furniture. Here, clearly, were targets that might be imitated by people with new money and some envy of their social superiors. Mimicking the aristocracy might be an early case of using consumerism to keep up with the Joneses (an early twentieth-century phrase applied to suburban American consumerism) – but in this case, the Sir Joneses.

It is impossible to argue away a certain amount of emulation, just as human nature and shopkeeper manipulation cannot be entirely dismissed. But historians deeply involved with early modern consumerism do not, in the main, accept this initial causation package as satisfactory. We have already discussed limits on the human nature argument. Commercial manipu-lation is a bit tougher, and we will have to deal with it at all stages and places of modern consumerism. For the eighteenth century, it can certainly be argued that the commercial inducements, while undeniably new and ingenious, simply cannot be used to explain deeply felt consumer needs. Lively prose in weekly newspapers might spark interest, but it hardly accounts for the passion that some people invested in new goods. Some avid consumers, including women, were not necessarily great readers at all, and so did not encounter advertisements directly. (Indeed these were most often aimed at men at this point.) Here is the general question: are large groups of people ever so sheep-like that commercial wiles can explain their consumer zeal (as opposed to explaining an interest in particular products)? And here is the first stage of consumerism question: were the new methods adequate to explain why some people would pass down a dress or a teapot with loving care, clearly believing it had deep emotional meaning beyond its material form?

Concerning the aristocracy: most of the people who bought new clothing or house wares in the eighteenth century – most ordinary consumers, in other words – did not mimic aristocratic styles. Most of them, indeed, had little or no direct contact with the aristocracy such that they could know what aristocratic styles were. We have seen that advertisers sometimes invoked aristocrats to call attention to a new product such as a razor strop. Aristocratic cachet surely counted for something, and people who bought new clothes may well have thought they were rising up the social ladder. But they did not seek, through consumerism, to become aristocrats. Their earnings were not great enough in the first place, and there is simply no widespread indication that their motives pointed in that direction in any event. There were aspirant aristocrats among some very wealthy merchants, but their methods involved purchasing country estates, aristocratic positions in government or church bureaucracies, or noble titles outright. Buying Wedgwood china or a bright cotton dress was not relevant.

There is, to be sure, a more subtle variant of the aristocracy argument. New consumers were not trying to ape the aristocracy. But they did resent aristocratic eminence, and they knew that, in the eighteenth century, aristocrats were in fact closing ranks, making entry more difficult than it had been before. So they sought alternative means of expression, through consumerism, not to pretend to be aristocrats but to demonstrate their worth, and that of their class, in a separate manner. This explanation, however, is more complicated than the simple emulation argument, and fits better with the more complex approaches discussed in the next section.

In sum: consumerism developed in a context in which new goods and commercial methods were in play, and in which new money earnings were available to large groups of people (though not to everyone). Upper-class consumer habits may have sparked some interest if not in specific forms of consumerism, at least in using consumer acquisition to make one's own mark in a hierarchical society. Again, some analysts might stop there, even arguing that these factors are more than sufficient to explain the changes that actually occurred. But the most challenging explanations do go further. Some of their apologists actually deny portions of the first set of causes, such as aristocratic emulation. Others admit them but downplay them, arguing that the crucial factors must be sought in more complex cultural and social shifts.

One possible factor was NOT heavily involved: explicit government sponsorship of consumerism. Writings about economics became more common during the eighteenth century. Many authorities urged governments to encourage population growth or to expand production for export, as means of strengthening the state. These measures might promote economic change, but they had virtually nothing to do with personal habits or even with distribution systems. Better banking facilities and new attention to transportation systems may have been more relevant, though we will see that, indirectly, population growth might play a role as well. But political causation ranks low on the list for the advent of modern consumerism. Later on, consumerism would have greater political connection, but not at this point. For the moment, governments thought far more in terms of war than of consumerism (still a competition in the world today), and they were also wedded to established hierarchies that consumerism might jeopardize. We've seen that individual rulers such as like Frederick the Great, for example, made correspondingly grumpy noises about new interests such as coffee-drinking. At most, governments stopped supporting sumptuary laws that might actively discourage consumer aspirations.

Accounting for new human needs

Two or three arguments attach consumerism to some of the larger but more subtle changes occurring in European society by the eighteenth century. Sometimes one of the arguments is developed independently – a very imaginative book by Colin Campbell thus focuses on culture alone. But it is also possible to combine the arguments in a persuasive picture.

The cultural approach

There is no question that European culture, including popular as well as elite beliefs, was changing rapidly by the eighteenth century. An obvious shift involved the Enlightenment. Enlightenment thinkers praised material progress. They focussed particularly on new tools and machines, rather than consumer goods, but they certainly supported a set of values consistent with believing that better clothing or furnishings constituted an acceptable goal in life. They stressed secular, rather than religious values, and for some people this change in itself may have helped legitimate greater consumer interests. They also often attacked the aristocracy as idle parasites, which might spur people to seek other ways to express an interest in material display. Finally, specific Enlightenment interests, such as the fervent belief that children could be improved through education, helped motivate middle-class purchases of items such as children's books and other pedagogical aids, which were becoming specific consumer categories by the end of the eighteenth century.

Many people, and not just the educated elite, had contact with Enlightenment ideas through reading or hearing others read pamphlets and essays.

The clearest result of this dissemination lay in the political sphere, with growing interest in political rights and even participation. But some seeds of consumerism may have been sown as well.

Despite this, the Enlightenment may not have been consumerism's chief cultural support. Along with this dominant intellectual movement came the early signs of another cultural current, ultimately called Romanticism. Romantic writers praised emotion and individualism. They talked of the importance of love and sorrow. They praised moral and physical beauty, and particularly female beauty. Colin Campbell argues that it was contact with these Romantic values, acquired especially through reading new, emotion-laden novels by English, French, and German authors that most explicitly spurred consumerism. People saw in consumerism a means of expressing their individual essence, and possibly also a way to stimulate love. In a century that increasingly emphasized women's responsibility for beauty, the association of consumerism with love and sexuality might affect this gender particularly. In related fashion, an increasingly emotional definition of family life – the family as center of affection – could undergird an interest in new objects that would decorate the family home and convey tenderness. Material objects, emotionalism and a new sense of self intertwined, and the early Romantic writings laid the foundation.

Of course, neither Enlightenment nor Romanticism, nor even a combination of the two, captured everyone. As we have seen, the eighteenth century also saw the rise of strict new religious movements, such as Methodism and Pietism, which focussed sharply on the spiritual side of life and discouraged vulgar display. But consumerism was not yet a universal behavioral code, so this qualification to the cultural argument poses no real problem.

The social approach

The eighteenth century was also the scene of massive social and economic changes, some of which had been brewing even before this point. In this approach, consumerism is seen particularly as a compensation for social changes, which, on their face, brought new levels of confusion, and a strong potential for loss of identity. There were new opportunities involved as well, and the social approach can also be combined with the idea of cultural reorientation. But the emphasis rests on consumerism as a means of countering potentially unfavorable changes or blurrings of social status.

The central development, again, was the ongoing commercialization of the West European economy, which by the eighteenth century was a long-established trend. Commercialization pushed many individuals, willingly or unwillingly, to challenge conventional social status. Merchants, obviously, might make considerable fortunes, so that although they and their occupations were not upper-class, they had some upper-class power and attributes.

Master artisans, starting out as ordinary craftsmen working alongside the journeymen they employed in their shops, might expand their operations and become, in essence, small manufacturers. If successful, they might stop working with their hands and begin to treat their journeymen as employees, not as fellow skilled workers. Here was a confusion of status for all parties involved, masters and journeymen alike.

Similar developments occurred in the countryside. Ambitious peasants might expand their landholdings, seeking to profit from new opportunities to sell grain or livestock on the market. They would in the process distance themselves from ordinary peasants, again confusing status markers on both sides of the divide. Rural manufacturing workers constituted a classic case of status confusion. These were the people who spun thread, wove cloth, or made small metal objects or shoes while working in their homes, with largely traditional, hand-operated equipment. They had little or no land, but they could, in good times, make a living through their productive labor – sometimes, doing better than the peasants around them. Where did they rate in the village pecking order? Not only social status, but age was involved here, as many of the workers were young, earning wages despite the fact that they had not inherited much from their parents.

Status disruptions were supplemented by two other developments. The first involved the spread of urban influences, a process clearly visible by the late seventeenth century. Urban populations were not yet growing much as a percentage of the total, but urban contacts were radiating from cities large and small. The spread of manufacturing to the countryside, or simply the sale of farm products to the cities, prompted many rural residents to travel periodically to urban centers, while urban agents fanned out in the farm areas to distribute raw materials and collect finished products in the manufacturing operation. This new web of contacts brought new exposure to urban styles and values, and helps explain the pattern of disseminating consumerism. Farm families gradually picked up some of the urban interests in tea and coffee sets, for example. Rural manufacturing workers (in contrast, at least for a time, to their more purely agricultural neighbors) eagerly assimilated urban clothing styles.

New opportunities for money making combined, in other words, with a shakeup of established social relationships and a wider network of urban contacts. This not only facilitated consumerism – the moneymaking part – but also motivated it as a way to establish status and personal identity in a rapidly changing social environment.

The second supplementary development, beginning around 1730 throughout most of Western Europe, featured rapid population growth: this also affected conventional markers of social status. Between 1750 and 1800, population in countries such as Britain and Prussia literally doubled, an unprecedented surge. Population growth created hosts of disruptions and hardships, of course. It also furthered the process of status change. More people had to rely on rural manufacturing in order to survive, for there was not enough land to go around. The hold of tradition, and the power of family supervision, declined for many young people. Parents could no longer guarantee land or artisanal jobs to all their children, who had to fend for themselves, usually in the wage labor market. They might survive, and sometimes even succeed, but they were cut off from the established badges of adult achievement.

And here is where consumerism fits in, for many ordinary people. If a person could demonstrate modest achievement in new ways, it could compensate for the disruption of the traditional channels. The trade-off could be quite direct: I was not able to become a skilled artisan, as there are not enough positions to go around, but I am making a money wage in domestic manufacturing. Since I cannot qualify for the traditional costume of an established craft – the fancy ceremonial clothing and badges worn by members of a guild – I will buy and wear vivid new clothing styles instead. And, of course, I know about these styles because of my contacts with urban people, and the styles are becoming more available given expanding production of cotton cloth, which is cheaper and also easier to dye in bright colors than the more traditional wool or linen. I feel that I am expressing myself and my identity through the new clothing, and am certainly distinguishing myself from my more conventional neighbors including (often) my parents and aunts and uncles. Finally, if the new clothing helps me win romance with the opposite sex (for many of the new consumers were also eager participants in changing habits of love and sexuality), so much the better.

The argument here is that changing social lines, resulting from commercialization and then population growth, invested the acquisition of new items, particularly clothing but also household amenities, with particular meaning. The items might be pleasant in themselves, but they served additional functions as badges of identity in a rapidly changing social climate. This explanation obviously highlights the differential spread of the new consumer habits. Young people picked up consumerism, particularly in clothing, faster than older adults. Domestic manufacturing workers adopted them well before their ordinary peasant neighbors, who could still be invested in the older symbols of achievement such as land ownership. Finally, the role of consumerism in status change was widely noted by observers at the time. From the eighteenth and into the mid-nineteenth century, many middle- and upper-class observers pointed out (usually as a complaint about deteriorating popular morals) that it was becoming impossible to tell a person's social status from the way he or she dressed. This was an exaggeration, of course; given wide gaps in earnings, people were hardly wearing the same quality of clothing across class lines. But clothing styles were democratizing, as new, often urban fashions cut across social divides.

The social approach and gender

Changes in gender relations involved some similar patterns of disruption, again related to the broad process of commercialization. The issue of gender and consumerism is complex, and we will be dealing with it in many settings in modern world history. It is vital to avoid an over simple association of women with consumerism; from the first, men could be avid consumers too, and they dominated some of the new consumer arenas such as coffee houses. But two aspects of the first phase of modern consumerism did have a disproportionate relationship to women. First, the new interest in household items such as tableware related to novel rituals of family dining, which were under women's control. The items created more domestic work for women, to be sure, but it also gave them power in the household – the prosaic but daily power of calling the family to dinner in a consumer-enriched setting.

Second, while both sexes enjoyed new clothing styles, the eighteenth century marked the first time in Western history that women were being clearly singled out as more beautiful, potentially at least, than men. Traditionally, it had been the upper class that was expected to embody beauty, and upper-class men had often been more concerned with beauty and dress than their female counterparts. But now, amid the growing interest in new clothing styles, it was women who headed the parade. Again, this was a mixed blessing at best. It involved women in new constraints and obligations – many of which have persisted and intensified even to the present day. But it also gave them new opportunities for self-expression, consumerist-style.

Finally, of course, there are hints, admittedly vague, that consumer items did mean more to women than to men. One historian has compared the wills of English men and women, from several social classes. This significance of wills as evidence now must be calculated along gender lines. Women were more likely to bequeath specific items – furnishings, tableware, and a prized dress – to equally specific female relatives, whereas men would consign their possessions to an heir without singling out particulars. The difference suggests that some women invested particular emotional value in their consumer belongings and sought to convey that value to an emotionally-prized relative: I want niece Sally to have my fancy chest of drawers because I love the chest and I love Sally and the association will have special meaning to me. Men committed to this kind of thinking more rarely, at least at this stage in modern consumer history.

From the sixteenth century onward, the position of women had been open to new debate in Western Europe. Protestantism, in the areas it affected, emphasized women as family members, for the religious orders where Catholic women could exist outside family were abolished. In the sphere of work, growing competition in a commercial environment prompted certain groups of male workers to try to shunt women aside. In the urban crafts, particularly, previous opportunities for women to become skilled workers and operate guilds were steadily curtailed. Many women still worked, of course. In rural families their labor was essential, and the spread of domestic manufacturing actually gave women new opportunities. But the association of women with family intensified, and opportunities to establish a mark outside a family context diminished – even in many Catholic areas.

Here was a setting in which women might be eager to use consumer opportunities to gain new interests and personal meaning. Here was a setting in which those aspects of budding consumerism that established women as objects of beauty (with clothing to match) and regulators of consumer-enriched family rituals could make sense, to women and men alike. Again, explaining consumerism as compensation for complex changes in status and function adds measurably to our capacity to understand some of the particular patterns involved.

Conclusion: loose ends

The arrival of modern consumerism is no mystery. It resulted from a number of factors operating concurrently, from new products and new earnings to new needs, framed by changing culture including growing urban influence. Disputes continue about specifics, such as the role, if any, of emulating the aristocracy. And the mix of factors can be vigorously debated. Certainly there was no tidy, single cause for such a complex change. Many historians, furthermore, would disagree with the presentation in this chapter, as it ultimately gives special emphasis to initial consumerism as social compensation. Some place greater emphasis on the drawing power of the new commercial apparatus – shopkeeping and advertisement; and some look more to the cultural changes associated with early Romanticism. There is ample room for questioning and a real need for further analysis. Nevertheless, a number of key components are clear, and they help not only explain the emergence of consumerism but improve the definition of its meaning to the people involved.

Several other issues remain. One involves both the range and intensity of early consumerism. The causes discussed above are so compelling that it may be tempting to assume that consumerism was more deeply rooted in the eighteenth century than in fact it was. As the previous chapter has already suggested, we do not know exactly how many people were caught up in consumer interests, or with what degree of commitment. The causes themselves help us differentiate certain groups. Urban people were more quickly and thoroughly involved than rural. Rural areas in contact with cities changed faster than rural areas in general. Young people moved toward consumerism faster than their older relatives, setting up a special relationship between advances in consumerism and youth culture that persists into the twenty-first century. People engaged in more secular cultural interests were more open than those attracted to religious fervor. The involvement with consumerism, clearly, was differentiated by setting and, doubtless, by individual personality as well.

Furthermore, even for groups it touched, consumerism was not yet so profoundly anchored that it could not be displaced by other concerns. The early industrial revolution, developing between the 1780s and 1840s first in Britain, then in other parts of Western Europe, provided a striking example. Simply put, the new workers in the factories, who might have been popular consumers par excellence, turned out to value other goals more strongly for several decades.

The process worked as follows. New factory workers were recruited from the ranks of former peasants, domestic manufacturers, and artisans. Many of them, in their backgrounds, would have been familiar with the kinds of consumerism that had developed in the eighteenth century. They were also disproportionately young, another favorable factor. Most important, they were involved in work that did not have clear status, but yielded a money wage. Factory work was often less skilled than artisanal labor, but it might pay better. Factory workers were often scorned by better-established urban residents. Here was a context in which consumerism might easily be used to demonstrate achievement and identity.

And, to an extent, it was. Factory workers did show an interest in clothing, prompting critics to note again how difficult it was to see who was really a worker by the outfits factory hands wore on Sunday, as they walked the city streets. And a few other items won attention, such as store-bought forks. But factory workers did not stake out a new level of consumerism, and they clearly placed other goals above consumer gains.

Some of the constraints were monetary. Many workers were paid badly, many suffered from periodic layoffs and other uncertainties. Costs of city housing and even food could eat into budgets. The margin for consumerism was small, sometimes nonexistent.

But there was more involved. In an unfamiliar setting, many workers chose leisure interests, even ones that cost some money, that were not primarily consumerist. They preferred to socialize with their colleagues in cheap bars than to spend on more explicitly consumer items. The value of comradeship, in a strange environment, and for some the numbing qualities of drink, took precedence. The formation of working-class singing groups and other organizations again showed the need for reconstructing social networks, above personal or familial consumerism.

More explicitly still: first-generation factory workers did not seek to maximize their money earnings, as would have been the case if acquisition held first place in their scheme of things. When workers were offered a higher wage, because of the skill level they had attained or because of a surge in business, they almost always reduced the time they spent at work rather than seizing the opportunity to improve their material standard of living. What they were saying, however implicitly, was quite clear. Their main problems involved unpleasant aspects of the new work setting, including noise, being bossed around by foremen, and having to work at the strenuous pace of the new, steam-driven machinery. If a higher wage gave them a bit of margin, they used the margin to regain personal, leisure time, not to compensate through a further consumerist burst. For workers, in other words, early industrialization set consumerism back. This reminds us that the causes of early consumerism, however compelling, did not necessarily carry everything or everyone before them. Workers would later become more ardent consumerists, but this would require a further set of causes that we will return to in dealing with consumerism's second phase.

Finally, what is the relationship between the initial causes of modern consumerism in Western Europe and the later spread of consumerism worldwide? Here, there are three points to keep in mind. First, after Western Europe achieved its initial version of a consumer society, it provided a model for other regions to imitate (or to disdain). The existence of European consumerism, in other words, added to the causes for consumerism elsewhere. Europe was clearly the most powerful region in the world; Europeans were expanding their commercial and colonial presence almost everywhere; the temptation to see the signs of European consumerism as signs of success to be imitated would be widely felt. All this could simplify causation.

Second: imitation of European consumerism did not mean that other societies would not generate their own causes for consumerist interest, and some of these could easily overlap with those experienced in Europe. Changes in culture, the development of new marketing methods, and status shifts for which acquiring new goods might compensate are ingredients we will see in other instances of consumerism. So though the European pattern was unique in one sense – it did not develop with any other fully consumerist model available for imitation – the causes involved deserve wider attention.

But third: societies outside Europe would have their own mix of factors, that would speed, delay or shape consumerism distinctively. Even the United States, so close to European conditions in many ways, would take some distinctive turns because of unusual cultural features including a deeper commitment to religion.

Modern consumerism gains greater meaning through exploring its causes. This is particularly true for the first outcropping of the phenomenon, where the causes were by definition particularly compelling and where debate among historians has centered. But attention to causes cannot be confined to this first case. Even in Western Europe, the further development of consumerism, particularly after the disruption of early industrialization, highlighted some additional factors that will be central to later analysis.

Further reading

In addition to the citations in Chapter 2: Colin Campbell, *The Romantic Ethic and The Spirit of Modern Consumerism* (Oxford: Basil Blackwell, 1987). On eighteenth-century economics and state policy: Isabel Hull, *Sexuality, State, and Civil Society in Germany, 1700–1815* (Ithaca, NY: Cornell University Press, 1996).

Chapter 4

Consumerism across the Atlantic

An early imitation

It may seem strange to realize that American consumerism was initially an imitation, but such was the case historically. The colonies that ultimately became the United States had to copy consumerism from Western Europe, and there is some debate about how fast they did so. Ultimately of course the United States would become a consumer giant, a world leader, but this chapter deals with the earlier, derivative phase. A number of factors help explain why the American colonies participated in modern consumerism with a bit of delay and hesitation.

At the same time, it was noteworthy that Americans were prepared to imitate so early. As we will see, no other society seized on the consumer revolution nearly as readily. This means there is another causation challenge, in explaining why the American colonies and then the new United States were such quick studies, generating a society only slightly behind European consumer levels and interests by 1850.

Imports: gewgaws and values

The Atlantic colonies of North America were closely tied to Western Europe, particularly England, in trade. They were generating some commercial wealth, mainly through products such as tobacco and furs, sold to Europe. Cultural links were close as well, on the part of white settlers. It was hardly surprising that Europe's exploding consumerism spilled across the ocean. Some historians of America, borrowing terminology from the recent work on Europe, have talked of a consumer revolution in the eighteenth century.

One group drawn to European consumer items was particularly unexpected: Native Americans along the seaboard and inland on key river ways. It is widely known, of course, that both French and English explorers triggered an extensive fur trade with Native Americans, buying pelts that could be sold back in Europe for considerable profits. (Beaver pelts were particularly popular, for hats.) An obvious question arises: the Native Americans involved were pressured but not forced (unlike their counterparts in the European-sponsored labor systems in Latin America at the same time). They worked either for money or for barter in European goods. The obvious question is: what were their motives? And the answer was a form of consumer interest.

As early as 1679 a European observer was noting that Native Americans had discovered "many Things that they wanted not before because they never had them." Trade had made them "become necessary for their use and ornament." The Native Americans were not gullible, at least not after an initial encounter. They did not want mere baubles, and they did not like some of the more cumbersome European fashions, including some men's trousers cut so tight that it was difficult to prepare to relieve oneself. But they did seek, and eagerly, an array of items ranging from cloth blankets to iron kettles to fancy coats – as well as, of course, metal knives and guns initially entirely new to them. Many of these items, including the textile products, were simply superior in utility or comfort to locally made goods. But there was also a taste for beauty that opened interests in beads, mirrors, and jewelry. Mirrors became a necessity, for men particularly, who could now dress and paint themselves without depending on women's help. "If they had a mirror before their eyes, they would change their appearance every quarter of an hour," wrote one scornful Englishman. Such was the extent of trade that many native crafts either disappeared or were transformed beyond recognition by European standards.

Native Americans were not, of course, ultimately the main bearers of American consumerism; their attraction was a temporary, though vital, episode. Their own economy declined by the later eighteenth century, because they had reduced the supply of too many of the most sought-after animals. Their very consumerism forced many into debt, which curtailed their capacity to continue to spend. Many, further, were gradually or abruptly driven westward by European settlers, unable to maintain the consumer interest or contact. Finally, by the late eighteenth century there was also an internal reaction, by Indian leaders who felt that their values and culture were being eviscerated. Many religious authorities began to urge not only a revival of older ceremonies, but also a deliberate severing of the trade with whites.

In the end, the burst of Native American consumerism is important in showing the power of new goods in rousing interest (as when Europeans encountered Asian goods, but here with even more potential because of the greater gap in prior material levels), but also the capacity of consumerism to undercut traditional identities and ultimately to fail. Native American communities in the nineteenth and twentieth centuries would be noteworthy for their incomplete acceptance of American consumer values, though of course individuals might choose to integrate more fully with the mainstream.

It was white Americans who provided the longer-lasting basis for American consumerism, and in this group as well important developments occurred during the eighteenth century. Here too, new European goods proved widely appealing. While the full shopkeeper apparatus of Western Europe did not yet emerge – advertising, for example, was more limited, despite a widely literate population – the number of stores did increase, along with increasingly aggressive marketing techniques, and peddlers mined the more remote areas. A sense of new necessities developed, particularly among people of middle income in the cities, as well as among Southern planters. An English visitor to Baltimore noted that "As wealth and population increased, wants were created, and many considerable demands, in consequence, took place for the various elegancies as well as the necessities of life." Of the consumer items current in Europe, certain food luxuries, and particularly tea and coffee, plus the array of tableware and selected household furnishings gained ground most extensively. Clothing fashions and related products had an audience as well, but there were fewer changes than in Europe. American consumer spending had a family context, which made the new household goods particularly relevant. It was in the home as well that some of the new ideas of comfort were shared with the Europeans. But there was some openness to fashion. An article in the Boston *Gazette* in 1763, by a "Countryman," told of the difference between a traditional homemade coat with horn buttons and the new insistence on "English-made cloth that cost . . . a guinea a yard." Somewhat more generally, another American talked about how New York, through its "intercourse with the Europeans," now followed the London fashions which in turn "introduced a degree of luxury in tables, dress and furniture, with which we were before unacquainted."

There was resistance as well, for this was an imported consumerism, not initially native-grown nor indeed nourished by much local manufacturing. There were some standard laments, about people spending beyond their means and challenging social hierarchy. A New Jersey minister, traveling into the back country, objected to the mirrors, pewter spoons and teapot in one log cabin: these should be sold to create savings for a rainy day, for ordinary people should not strive for fancy items. Not surprisingly, shock was even greater when slaves could occasionally display some interest in fashionable clothing. Even aside from "uppity" slaves, traditionalists found enough consumerism around them to sound alarms – again, echoing European debate. The frenzy for new goods defied appropriate hierarchy – "the lowest rank of men would pass for a middle sort; and every one lives above his condition," one critic noted; "Thus a whole nation falls to ruin." Not surprisingly, commentary here, as in Europe, took on a gendered town: women were accused of frivolity, while consumerist men seemed effeminate. There were some special concerns as well, as tensions with Britain mounted. Critics referred to the new goods as "Baubles of Britain" and found their luxury "effeminating." In an increasingly tense political environment, the economic dependence on Britain that the first American consumerism created was also attacked. These comments, of course, were double-edged: they showed concern about consumerism but also its presence; they demonstrated anti-British sentiment but also the increasing flood of imports, particularly of household items but also some clothing, on which growing colonial consumerism depended.

Viewpoints directly clashed during the 1760s, when protests against British taxation and other policies mounted. Various patriotic groups tried to organize consumer boycotts of British goods. A number of groups, including associations of "young ladies," pledged to stop buying or using imported products such as tea. A more general prohibition list suggested the range of goods American consumerism already involved: "Silks, Velvets, Clocks, Watches, Coaches, and Chariots." The movement was serious, but it initially failed. Too many merchants relied on the sales of imports, and too many people wanted the goods. But leaders who insisted on a higher morality, in the context of the disputes with Britain, returned to the charge. In 1774 the First Continental Congress established local committees to guard against imports. As a "Carolinian" put it:

> We need only fight our Own selves, suppress for a while our Luxury and Corruption, and wield the Arms of Self Denial in our own Houses, to obtain the Victory . . . And the man who would not refuse himself a fine Coat, to save his Country, deserves to be hanged.

This final pre-revolutionary boycott was not, of course, a durable rebellion against consumerism, despite the interesting association of luxury and corruption. Yet it does raise questions about the extent of American consumerism at this point, compared to European.

Causes and further changes

Most people in the soon-to-be United States were rural; the percentage of population in the cities was considerably smaller than in Europe. Many dealt only rarely in money. Material standards were high, on average, because of a favorable ratio of people to resources. This showed in relatively abundant food, in high life expectancy and high birth rates compared to European norms. The result was not, however, precocious consumerism. The American economy was largely non-commercial; the southern plantations, the main exception to this, did not provide funding for substantial participation in import consumerism save for the handful of planters and their families themselves. Most people bartered for the goods and services they needed, such as building a home or clearing a field or milling grain. It was only in the later eighteenth century that many people, even those with some means, acquired housing that had more than two or three rooms. This was not an environment compatible with the level of consumerism that was developing in Western Europe.

There were two other constraints. First, the causes of European consumerism, though present in the American context, were simply not as well developed. This refers not only to the absence of a full range of shops and shopping lures, but also to the fact the Americans were not faced with the erosion of traditional social and gender standards to the same extent as their European cousins. The very absence of a substantial commercial economy reduced the threats to established status and identity; and while American women faced change and various inferiorities, their work roles were far more fundamental than was true by this point in Europe. Consumerism as compensation, in other words, was less salient. Second, American culture, with its strong religious emphasis, supplemented now by a nationalistic desire to preach American virtue against European corruption, was less fully attuned to the possibility of consumerism than was the case in Europe.

There is no need simply to speculate about the limits to American consumerism. There is direct evidence, despite the undeniable signs of consumerist advances during the eighteenth century. While a few clocks and watches were imported in the eighteenth century, for example, their use was not yet widespread. They were a rarity before about 1815 in the wealthy Hudson River valley, towns and countryside alike. On another front: the passion for second-hand clothing, and the rate of clothing thefts, so indicative of consumer values in Britain, simply had no wide echo in the United States before the 1820s. The point is clear. The colonies that became the United States participated in Europe's first consumer revolution as imitators but with a definite lag. A real revolution of this sort had yet to occur on American shores. There was change and there were new interests, on the part of various Americans, but there was also explicit hostility provoked by the foreign and artificial origins of the new behaviors.

The hesitations were temporary, of course. The American economy did become rapidly more commercial after about 1800. Use of money expanded dramatically, in the market-oriented countryside as well as in the growing cities. Even as politics became more democratic, social and gender distinctions grew. This created new opportunities to use consumer goods to establish separate identity or to react against otherwise demeaning forms of social change. Purchase of watches expanded because time became more important, but also for display. A gold watch (now made in the United States, where production of timepieces expanded rapidly after 1808 and where peddlers carried the goods widely) "combines embellishment and utility in happy proportions and is usually considered a very valuable appendage for the gentleman," trumpeted an article in the Hudson valley *Rural Repository* in 1833.

American parlors began to fill with store-bought furniture in the same period, as a badge of family respectability and success. Pioneered by the urban middle class, ornamental parlors spread to successful farmers, artisans, even immigrants (Italian-Americans would still be relying on parlors after 1900). They were filled not only with stiff, decorative chairs, but also lamps, imported oriental rugs, and other items. As in Western Europe, the piano became a family consumer good of the highest importance. Despite its considerable expense, the piano was seen as a center of family sociability and respectable female accomplishment. Household consumerism, in other words, was intensifying.

But American consumerism now went outside the home as well. It was in the 1840s that French fashions and also French restaurants began to take the urban upper class by storm. While most Americans stuck to a hearty but non-consumerist diet of meat and potatoes (in great quantity, typically eaten very fast), a wealthy minority began to indulge in many courses of imported luxuries. Women's fashions constituted an even more important marker. Magazines such as *Godey's Ladies Book* began to reproduce the latest French styles in ways that would allow women of more modest means to sew their own copies and become paragons of an up-to-date look in their own right.

An interest in consumerism, particularly in clothing, began to attract some elements of the lower classes. For example, African American river-boat workers, freer than most African Americans prior to Emancipation, took a delight in relatively fancy dress and gold ornaments. They earned enough to afford these modest luxuries, which also served to set them off from the common images associated with slavery. In turn, this commit-ment to a consumerist "sporting life" contrasted with the religious fervor that was also present in African American ranks.

Clearly, the initial, imitative phase of American consumerism had set the base for more rapid development later on, in the second quarter of the nine-teenth century. A partially imitative quality remained: Americans continued to find Europe a model of consumer standards (but also a potential source of corruption). A sense of national consumerist leadership was yet to come. But now the embrace was bringing Americans of appropriate means close to European standards – and farmers, more active in market agriculture than most European peasants, may indeed have moved ahead in rural consumerism.

This raises the final analytical question: why did American consumerism, delayed for important reasons, take off as rapidly as it did? Close contact with European, and particularly British, trade and culture, including a grudging sense of inferiority to Europe in the finer things of life, provides part of the answer. This spurred the preparatory imitation of the eighteenth century, with the flood of consumer imports, which in turn helped set the basis for more rapid developments later on. Some American consumerism sought to compensate for a sense that the United States was more back-ward than Europe, and needed a more stylish approach through consumer copying or innovation or both. The United States had also participated extensively in the Enlightenment, which as in Europe brought greater openness to secular interests; Romantic novels, often imported from Britain, also spread widely.

Furthermore, in the nineteenth century, rapid social and economic change created some of the same needs for consumerism as a source of identity and compensatory satisfaction as had occurred in Europe slightly earlier. Particularly by the second quarter of the nineteenth century, when American consumerism began to pick up, new types of immigrants and the process of urbanization both spurred concerns about identity that consumerism could answer. Urbanites, in particular, were eager to distinguish themselves from country bumpkins. Some immigrants also hoped to use consumer advance to demonstrate that their long journey had been worthwhile. African American interest reflected a desire to use consumerism to fight stereotypes of inferiority. At the same time, however, traditionalist resistance to consumerism was harder to come by in the United States than in Europe. Social distinctions were never as firm in the United States as they had customarily been in Europe, save for minority races. The class-blurring, partially democratic implications of consumerism could advance quite rapidly in this context. Criticisms of fashionable clothing for erasing class distinctions were less common in the United States than in Europe, for precisely this reason. Here, as with the rapid expansion of the commercial economy and the sheer size of the American market, were potent spurs to American consumerism once it did come into its own.

The set of factors that promoted consumerism overlapped between Europe and the United States. But the American mix was just slightly distinctive, which explains some differences in timing but also ultimately set American consumerism on a particularly rapid course. By 1850 it begins to be possible to talk of European and American consumerism in almost the same breath. By 1880 it begins to be possible to delineate areas of American consumer leadership, as the pupil began teaching the master.

Further reading

Early American consumerism is actually understudied. Several important articles appear in Lawrence Glickman, ed., *Consumer Society in American History: A Reader* (Ithaca, NY: Cornell University Press, 1999). On change: Alan Kulikoff, *The Agrarian Origins of American Capitalism* (Charlottesville: University Press of Virginia, 1992), Richard Bushman, *The Refinement of America. Persons, Houses, Cities* (New York: Vintage Books, 1992), Christopher Clark, *The Roots of Rural Capitalism* (Ithaca, NY: Cornell University Press, 1990), and above all T.H. Breen, *The Marketplace of Revolution: How Consumer Politics Shaped American Independence* (New York: Oxford University Press, 2004).

Chapter 5

The explosion of consumerism in Western Europe and the United States

We have seen that a consumer revolution occurred in the eighteenth century, and that it carried the seeds of geographical expansion, particularly in the impact on the United States. Development then slowed for a bit, as Western Europe assimilated the first stages of the industrial revolution and the United States caught up with European consumerist standards. A second stage of consumerism subsequently burst forth from about 1850 onward. The theme was simple but profound: in virtually every conceivable way, consumerism accelerated and intensified on both sides of the Atlantic. This chapter traces this process, which also proved vital to consumerism's larger world impact.

The story has a number of highlights. The apparatus of consumerism changed, as shops and wordy advertisements were increasingly replaced by new retail outlets and a still-more manipulative advertising style. The range of goods involved expanded to include the first "consumer durables" – big ticket items, compared to the clothing and furniture interests that of course persisted as well. Leisure entered the consumer orbit for the first time in any full sense. And the human needs expressed in consumerism also changed, as the process of acquisition and accumulation began to address a wider range of problems. Even the nature of consumerist theft changed, as a sign of intensification.

There were continuities, of course, for modern consumerism has some standard features. Some historians who have worked on the eighteenth-century revolution have tended to assume that consumerism, once launched, simply developed along lines of inevitability. But this new stage is sufficiently different that it must be separately treated. And it must also be separately explained, in part at least: what caused people to stake more on consumerism than they had in the earlier, more exploratory phase?

Finally, this chapter treats a few other interpretive issues. Gender is one. More clearly than in the initial phase, consumerism began to be pinned on women. The attribution was inaccurate, but it must be addressed. Social class and race formed other consumerist factors, though as always some aspects of consumerism blurred social divisions.

The time period treated in this chapter is a long one. Early symptoms of consumerism's intensification emerged before 1850. The symptoms accelerated fairly steadily into the 1920s, when much of the characteristic contemporary apparatus of consumerism was either fully established or at least clearly sketched. There would be further change even in the transatlantic home of modern consumerism, which we will pick up in a later chapter, but the implications of a fully developed consumer society were plainly visible by this point. Even the Great Depression of the 1930s would only interrupt the phenomenon, and incompletely at that.

Two final complexities require emphasis. In dealing with intensification, this chapter risks assuming a straightline development from the mid-nineteenth to the mid-twentieth century. This would be extremely misleading. A large number of groups were still too poor to participate significantly in consumerism, even after World War II. One estimate, for example, suggests that only five percent of all shopping in 1900 was done in department stores; the rest focussed on more conventional sales outlets, some of them more involved with necessities than with consumerist items. Major events often sidetracked consumerism as well: consumerism plummeted during the world wars (though more in Europe than in the United States). In Germany by 1917, avoiding hunger was a far more pressing daily goal for many people than consumerism was. There was a basic trend, but it was hardly uniform across the social hierarchy or across time.

Nor – and this was the final complexity – was it entirely uniform across place, even within the Western world. Continental West Europeans had more debates about consumerism than Americans or Britons did; there were more hesitations about some of the newest kinds of stores, that seemed to compete with worthy shopkeepers or that seemed to sacrifice artistic qualities for cheap price and debased mass taste. The fact that countries such as France still had large peasant populations, more attached to land than to consumerism, also caused differentiation. The United States, with its huge national market, was more conducive to mass advertising than most European countries were during most of this period. Common trends existed, particularly compared to many other parts of the world, but it is vital to avoid a sense of absolute homogenization. One of the reasons that mounting "Americanization" would seem so jarring to many Europeans after World War II was that American-style consumerism had not previously conquered the Western terrain.

The department store

Just as the shop heralded the first phase of consumerism, so the department store came to symbolize the second phase. More than symbols were involved: in the larger cities, themselves containing a growing minority of the overall population in the Western world, the department store was an active agent in extending consumerism and the aspirations and fantasies it could involve.

The first department store opened in Paris in the 1830s. It was really an agglomeration of clothing shops, clustered so that shoppers would have more to attract them. Gradually, department stores added a wider array of goods, such as kitchenware, furniture, and toys, though clothing and related items remained central.

The key to the department stores, besides the array of goods, was display and mass. Consumer items were laid out in profusion, deliberately designed to tempt the purchaser's appetite. This was the retail version of a factory, with items arranged with machine-like precision. The result was what one historian has called a "dream world" of material luxury. Materialism was the lure. Unlike the old-fashioned shop (which of course persisted, though amid great anxiety for the future), store clerks were instructed not to socialize. There was no easy familiarity, though clerks were also told how to manage customers to make them ready to buy.

However anonymous the atmosphere, department stores added important ingredients to the act of shopping. Many people now went to department stores as much for the experience as with any particular purchase in mind. Young couples might stroll through the store simply for recreation.

Department stores sedulously promoted novelty. Obviously they heralded new products and fashions, trying to persuade people that even if they had something, they should visit again for a newer model. Window displays were changed frequently, to associate products with holidays or other lures. Of course the stores advertised widely, but they also sought additional forms of promotion. Macy's, the great New York store, thus introduced the Thanksgiving Day parade in 1924, to call attention to Christmas buying on a day not usually associated with commercialism.

Department stores spread quickly from their Parisian origins. They could be found in most big cities in Western Europe and the United States by the 1850s. They even began to spread to Russia, and would later arise in other parts of the world as well. Clearly, consumerism had reached a stage where the number of goods and the range of appetites had combined to require a new retail palace.

The department store was not the only change in the apparatus of consumerism. In the United States, catalogs began to appear, designed for mail order sales to rural and small-town customers. The catalog offered an even broader range of goods than the department store, for a time including even prefabricated homes available from outlets such as Sears and Roebuck. Pictures in the catalog were not elaborate, but they added an eye-catching element, particularly in the fashion arena, that could draw rural people further into the consumer orbit.

Also from the United States, initially in the last decades of the nineteenth century, came the "dime store" – stores with cheap consumer items, including cosmetics and, often, some clothing, aimed at masses of urban buyers who needed better prices and more widespread locations than department stores offered. The stores provided access to some consumerism for elements of the urban lower classes. These kinds of stores spread fairly readily to Britain. On the continent, however, they encountered more resistance, partly because they were foreign, partly because – to critics – their products seemed not only cheap but tasteless. During the 1920s and 1930s considerable debate about these stores occurred in countries such as France, where new national chains – such as the Monoprix, or "single price," largely pre-empted foreign rivals and where owners could claim that they were paying more attention to style and to "Frenchness" than their English and American counterparts.

Advertising changed greatly. In the first place, explicit advertising agencies were launched. The United States headed the parade here too, in the 1870s; the first French agency would follow only in 1922. But even when expertise remained in-house, the nature of advertising shifted rapidly. New printing techniques involved more visual display. Colorful posters touted shows and products. Magazines offered alluring fashion poses, and even newspapers added product imagery. When words were used, they began to appear in bolder typeface, with a simplified text open to people whose literacy was shaky and designed to appeal to an emotional, more than a reasoned response. Furthermore, written texts themselves were altered to embrace more value-laden phrases, as opposed to more straightforward product descriptions. Silk goods, for example, were still discussed in utilitarian terms in newspaper ads as late as the 1890s; paragraphs would emphasize economical price, durability, and quality. But the tone changed by 1900: new silk stockings were "alluring," "bewitching" – "to feel young and carefree, buy our silk."

Advertising was not confined to conventional media. Certain products could be promoted through the growing school system. Thus soap companies, by the 1920s, managed to enlist school authorities in hygiene programs that would expand sales potential. During World War I, American cigarette companies distributed free goods to the troops, a patriotic gesture that won them favorable attention and also gave tens of thousands of former soldiers a lifelong habit.

Changes in media ultimately included the radio, a potent source of advertising that could reach directly into the home and also attract preliterate children, not only building their demands for particular childhood products but also converting them to a deep sense that consumerism was an appropriate expression whatever the age.

Other consumer apparatus developments included more extensive credit facilities. Americans, in particular, began to reduce their savings levels and accumulate more consumer debt by the early 1900s.

The question arises, of course, about the growing power of manipulation. To what extent were new levels of consumerism simply the result of the undeniable acceleration in the power to create demand? The question is harder to answer during this phase of consumerism than it was during the pioneering phase, precisely because the commercial appeals were more varied, sophisticated, and omnipresent. Most historians who have examined advertising conclude, however, that improvements in manipulation were not the whole story. Advertisements and department or chain store lures might persuade people to buy a particular product; they did not, by themselves, persuade them to increase their stake in consumerism more generally. Indeed, not all advertising campaigns succeeded. Advertisers often found that they were trying to determine existing values, around which they could base their appeals. The changes in the apparatus of consumerism were important; they had definite impact; but they still must be combined with the other factors involved.

Consumer goods

Needless to say, the array of consumer products expanded steadily. Sources included a widening array of imports, such as the rapidly-expanding silk industry in Japan or the fast-growing rug manufacturing in Turkey (including some factories as well as greater numbers of artisanal workers). But there were more consumer items produced in Western factories as well. Some of them benefited from entirely new materials, such as plastic (introduced around 1850), vulcanized rubber, photographic film, and (in the early twentieth century) artificial fibers such as rayon and nylon.

By 1900, many companies had research units designed to introduce consumer product modifications. Chemical companies in Germany pioneered this approach, but it spread rapidly. Some industrial research involved products destined for other business operations, such as fertilizers for commercial agriculture. But researchers also worked on consumer items. The result was not only new products, but also modifications of familiar staples so that the characteristic label "new and improved" could be tacked on. Many companies began building what came to be called "planned obsolescence" into their output. Automobiles became an expensive but successful case in point. After some effort to introduce standardized designs that would have the appeal of durability, car makers by the 1920s and 1930s began to introduce annual model changes, often largely cosmetic, that would persuade people that what they had purchased if not last year, at most three years before, was hopelessly out of date. The technique was not really new, for clothing fashions had involved the same principles of eager novelty. But now the approach was being applied more widely, to a greater range of products and to more expensive ones.

But it was the growing range of consumer goods that constituted the main point. Clothing and adornment continued to be important. Increasing sales of cosmetics, and new items such as deodorants, added to this list, particularly by the 1920s. Household furnishings commanded attention as well. The addition of the piano to the must-buy items, for middle-class homes, showed how innovation could swell this product category. By the later nineteenth century the advent of home appliances constituted yet another important and costly opportunity.

Food also drew consumerist attention. The habit of dining out in restaurants expanded gradually. The 1920s saw the introduction of working-class restaurants for pleasure, such as the fish and chips shops in England or, just slightly later, hamburger joints in the United States. Another revealing sign of food consumerism, particularly widespread in the United States, involved snacking. Commercial snack manufacture began in the 1880s, in the form of items such as crackers. Initially, the products were touted in terms of health – "convenient, palatable and healthful" foods that could be packed by "bicyclists, tourists and students"; they were also produced in clean surroundings. But over time the appeals became increasingly sensual: snacks should be consumed because they tasted good and there was no point in suffering a moment's hunger. Ancillary products also gained ground, such as chewing gum and, in the tobacco realm, the cigarette.

Transportation focussed growing consumer attention as well, spurred both by novel products and by the growing size of cities. The introduction of easily ridden bicycles launched a major craze in the 1870s and 1880s, in both Europe and the United States. Everyone in the middle class had to have one. Bicycle clubs formed, touring wide stretches of the countryside on both sides of the Atlantic and also pushing for better roads. Bicycle racing groups became a staple in Europe, often forming in association with a neighborhood bar. Bikes became integral to courtship, as couples could out-pedal any adult chaperones. As with the best consumer innovations, bicycles also prompted other changes in buying habits. Women, particularly, needed new clothes to ride a bike, and confining Victorian skirts yielded to less formal, more athletic gear.

But of course the big-ticket consumer item par excellence became the automobile, introduced around the turn of the century. Car purchases began at the top of the social scale but quickly spread downward, reaching American farmers by the 1910s and beginning to penetrate the working class soon thereafter. Even Hitler in Germany, not for the most part a promoter of consumerism, introduced the people's car, or Volkswagen, in the 1930s.

Consumer items destined for children also proliferated. Manufactured toy soldiers were a hot ticket around 1900, in various social groups. Dolls became more varied. The introduction of soft, cuddly animal dolls – including the teddy bear, named after President Theodore Roosevelt, though imitating earlier innovations in Germany – spread consumerism to the infant age bracket. Balls and other sports equipment spread widely among boys. Books were now written not only for children, but also for children as buyers, and parents did not always approve. Cheap, simple novels, called penny dreadfuls in England, featured adventure stories or westerns, and were designed for sheer escapism.

Consumerist leisure

One of the huge growth areas in this second phase of consumerism involved commercial leisure. The genre was not entirely new, of course, but now it virtually took command of the time not devoted to work or rest.

Traditionally, most leisure had involved customary group activities, for example festivals, or more spontaneous behaviors such as singing or chatting at work. These forms had declined with industrialization, because they interfered with the regularity of factory life. In their place, two major leisure forms developed: participant activities that often required consumer equipment, and spectator leisure, the consumerist form par excellence.

Consumer products now supplemented children's and adult play in many ways. Sports now demanded balls, mitts, and other store-bought products. Music benefited from the growing availability of instruments to interested purchasers. Dancing spread in commercial dance halls – there were sixty-eight halls in Paris by 1860. Eager tourists could now sign up for commercial tours, with agencies such as Thomas Cook (formed in England in the 1840s) or the American Express (1870s); and of course they could buy guidebooks. Day excursions to the beach, organized by train companies, brought commercial leisure travel even to the working class. Pictures from the 1880s show European workers crowding the beaches, dressed fairly formally both because specialized swimwear was another generation away (when it would become an important consumer item) and because most people did not know how to swim. But the beaches were soon surrounded by pleasure galleries in which people could supplement their exposure to nature by buying games, looking at freak shows, and snacking.

Commercial performances for spectators loomed even larger. Professional sports began to organize in the 1850s, and spread steadily. The first adult soccer football club formed in England in 1858, and leagues developed in the next decade. Professional baseball arose in the United States at about the same time. In addition to sport, popular music hall (called vaudeville in the United States) drew people from various social groups to watch singers, comics, and dance routines. These entertainment forms served as the basis for the first movies, which began to draw audiences around 1900. By 1920, the average American family was attending at least one movie a week, and Europeans were not far behind. Even newspapers promoted the new passion for leisure. They featured sports sections and entertainment sections, linked to advertising. But they also provided escapism on their own, by featuring a variety of human interest subjects such as titillating crimes, disasters or exotic items such as the Loch Ness monster. American papers also introduced the comic strip. People increasingly expected to be entertained by buying pleasure from commercial outlets – the essential definition of consumerist leisure. In the United States, the amusement park provided another widely popular source of consumerist leisure. The Ferris wheel was invented in the 1890s, and the roller coaster soon followed.

Even sex became a spectator sport in part. The advent of pornographic postcards spread sexual imagery more widely than ever before. Women's bodies, sometimes portrayed in exotic "native" settings, formed the prime subject matter here. Cheap novels used sexual themes as well as violence, a combination which quickly became a consumer staple. Sex was also increasingly linked to advertising. Some bars featured nudes in their outdoor signs, and products such as German Bitters, sold in the United States, had a bare-breasted woman in the background as early as 1885.

The triumph of consumerist leisure simultaneously transformed recreation and greatly extended the reach of consumerism overall. Few people in Western Europe or the United States, by 1900, did not expect to spend part of their day watching, reading or listening to some product designed to entertain them. This association of daily free time with consumer behavior was a first in human history.

Consumerist leisure extended another key quality of the whole phenomenon: the embrace of faddism. Just as fashions shifted, and car models changed, so did leisure enthusiasms. Dance styles oscillated with bewildering regularity. During the early twentieth century they went from the tango and waltz to the shimmy, then the Charleston and black bottom, then the one-step and the waltz again. Sports crazes followed one on the other, though some of the staples held on as well. In the United States the rise of baseball was challenged around 1900 by a new enthusiasm for American football. Popular songs and song styles changed regularly, and of course consumerist leisure generated a regular procession of sports and entertainment stars, taken up with great enthusiasm and then rejected with equal speed when another idol came along. Leisure, once associated with traditional continuity as the basis for community life, now reversed direction: change was essential, and what communities there were formed largely around these shifting commitments.

Audiences: democratization?

Consumerism steadily drew more and more groups of people into an increasing array of consumer orbits. Distinctions remained, partly of course because resources varied greatly. A middle-class vacation, or mode of transport, continued to differ greatly from comparable working-class items. Differences in styles based on prior cultures also shaped group choices. One historian has shown how, in the United States, different immigrant groups continued to patronize special food or fashion products that confirmed their group identity, even as they became increasingly consumerist.

Poverty and the uncertainty caused by frequent economic crises also created huge divisions in access to consumerism. People in working-class sections of London or Paris never made it to the fashionable department stores, and many had only infrequent engagement with consumerism of any sort. Many working-class and peasant families concentrated on saving money, if there was any margin, realizing that an increase in unemployment, a period of illness or the process of growing old would demand resources that must not be wasted on consumerism. In many lower-class families, women assumed the special burden of careful frugality – sometimes granting their husbands a bit of beer money to keep them away from more expensive habits. As late as 1946 a British observer, Charlotte Luetkens, noted that "Throughout the centuries, women have been taught the virtue of hoarding and saving – now they have to learn the art of spending."

Nevertheless, some patterns of change emerged, even though there was no uniformity. The growing reach of consumerism, and some homogenizing tendencies across group lines, showed in many ways. The idea of bathing regularly (with the latest advertised soap) and smelling good started in the middle class, but by 1900 it cut across class and ethnic lines. The school campaigns to promote hygiene deliberately sought to use children to press working-class parents to measure up to the best bathing and tooth-brushing standards. By 1930 soap was the second most common grocery item, after bread, to be found in the American home.

Various age groups were drawn in. Consumerism had long been associated with youth and young adulthood, and to some extent this continued: these were the age groups most interested in novelty and often blessed with the greatest disposable incomes. But consumerism also spread, as we have seen, into childhood and even babyhood. The proliferation of toys briefly worried some observers. "Why foster a craving for novelty and variety that life cannot satisfy?" But more experts approved: toys could give young children emotional support. As an American observer put it in 1914, "children's affections have come to center around the toys with which they have lived and played." Anxiety about toys and reading material that were purely entertaining, with no educational value, was largely relieved through buying children still more toys, but with a better cachet: many middle-class parents began to organize playrooms filled with goods – approved goods, but goods, nevertheless. The notion of comforting a young child by buying something new became a standard. Particularly in the United States, the growing middle-class practice of giving allowances, which began in the 1890s, helped create a child consumer market.

More tentatively, consumerism also spread upward in the age bracket. The elderly had never been seen as a consumerist group. This was a time of retrenchment and, often, greater poverty. But by the 1920s some consumer activities began to be organized for older people, including commercial tourism. The full development of consumerism for the elderly would not occur until the 1950s, but there were earlier hints, at least within the middle classes, for the phenomenon challenged more traditional group boundaries.

Obviously, consumerism spilled across class and ethnic lines. Many Jewish immigrants to the United States, for example, were quickly drawn in, eager to acquire new clothes and other items. One immigrant memoir featured a chapter, "Buy Now, Pay Later – Mama Discovers an American Custom." Consumerism might in fact help immigrants justify their risky commitment to a new land, both to themselves and, through letters and visits, to folks back home. African Americans participated in consumerism when their means permitted, particularly of course in the cities to which many moved during the great migration of the early twentieth century. Cosmetics were widely popular, some designed to make people look less African. But other consumer items featured black entertainers, particularly in the area of music and dance. Even in the nineteenth century a consumerist model for some African Americans had emerged in the model of the sportin' life: men, with women on their arms, dressed in eye-catching clothes and jewelry and up-to-date on the latest entertainment forms.

The involvement of the working class in full-blown consumerism, tempered mainly by still-insecure resources, was one of the key developments in this period. Workers did not accept middle-class consumer standards fully, even when they could afford them. But where resources permitted they did display a similar passion to acquire, and they often gradually compromised with middle-class standards. Movies proved a classic case in point. The violence and low comedy of many movies came from popular entertainment traditions. But specifically working-class themes did not prove durably popular, and middle-class characters predominated after 1920. Furthermore, working-class movie audiences, initially rowdy and noisy in the best popular spectator tradition, soon quieted, accepting other norms of respectability. Yet cross-class consumerist contacts could cut both ways. Many new middle-class commercial leisure interests resulted from patronizing working-class theaters or fashions. "Slumming" could provide an excitement that purely middle-class tastes did not satisfy.

Finally, consumerism continued to cross gender lines, particularly as women moved into consumer areas initially reserved for men. Tobacco smoking was an example: once a classic male consumer preserve, tobacco drew women increasingly after the introduction of the cigarette. Automobiles were initially targeted at men, but here too women's importance as consumers was increasingly recognized, among other things through greater attention to upholstery and design.

In all this, the purveyors of consumerism managed to expand their audiences while combining some common tendencies with special bows to the identities of particular age groups, ethnicities, or each gender. No audience was left untouched, though the rural segments, particularly in the West European peasantry, were drawn in most slowly and hesitantly.

Functions and needs

Attachments to consumerism escalated along with all the more measurable symptoms. A number of cultural forces, initially hostile to consumerism, now aligned themselves (though there was also new opposition, a point discussed in the following chapter). Protestant ministers in the United States had typically railed against the growing signs of consumerism in the first half of the nineteenth century. A minister in 1853 condemned excessive spending, "by the parade of luxury, in eating, drinking and dressing, and almost every indulgence of the flesh." "Man should aspire to more durable riches than those this world can offer." Vestiges of this sentiment continued, as in an attack from the 1870s:

> If we spent more time of Sabbath mornings in preparation of the heart than in the adornment of the person, might we not be better able to worship God in the beauty of holiness?

But mainstream Protestantism largely shifted ground, arguing that consumer goods, while not a top priority, were part of God's gifts to mankind. Thus the *Presbyterian Banner*, a religious weekly, actually began to criticize women who lacked a fashion sense:

> If a woman has no natural taste in dress, she must be a little deficient in her appreciation of the beautiful . . . Indifference, and consequent inattention to dress, often shows pedantry, self-righteousness, or indolence, and . . . may frequently be noted as a defect.

The paper at this point began accepting fashion ads and even offered a regular column on fashion and "the further importations of French Costumes." Enjoyment of material goods now demonstrated true religious spirit, as against "the accumulated mould of sourness." "When the angels have enlarged and purified your own heart, . . . they will thus secure to you the full unabridged edition of happiness in this world, as well as in world no. 2." "Enjoy the present . . . the blessings of this day if God sends them."

Evaluation of envy changed as part of this cultural shift, though the process took a bit longer, extending into the twentieth century. Moral authorities conventionally attacked envy as a petty symptom of a poor sense of priorities. Women's apparent eagerness to copy clothing from the upper classes, as in the growing interest in silk stockings, frequently drew adverse comment. Some of these blasts, even in the United States, reflected the longstanding hostility to use of consumerism to blur class lines. Thus working-class women were particularly (and inaccurately) condemned for frivolous spending. The new attachments of rural women to standards gleaned from catalogs were similarly chastised. People should "be content with what you have," as one Christian magazine put it in 1890. But the tone changed after about 1915. American women of all classes began to be congratulated for dressing so well: "Whatever their background, they seem all to be inspired with what we are told is a typical and standardized American desire to 'look like a million dollars.'" While there was vanity involved, most of it was "innocent . . . wholesale ambition to look one's best, to achieve beauty and distinction, to assert good taste and cultivated selection in clothes." Advertisers, indeed, began to praise envy directly: a soap ad thus asked, "The Envied Girl – Are you one? Or are you still seeking the secret of charm?" Virtue and vice thus were re-evaluated, and while some of this clearly resulted from the growing power and subtle tactics of commercial advertisers, there was a real culture shift as well.

Consumerism began to play a role in additional aspects of life. It penetrated most holidays. Americans began exchanging commercially-bought Christmas presents as early as the 1830s, and the focus steadily gained prominence. By the end of the century, Christmas buying was taking on huge proportions. Purchasing gifts was meant to convey family emotion. Valentine's Day had its own commercial apparatus. The first commercial cards were introduced in Britain for Valentine's Day in 1855. The idea of celebrating birthdays with consumer items was another innovation. After 1900, holidays began to be invented partly for consumerist purposes – but always with family meaning thrown in. Thus Mother's Day, proclaimed in the United States officially in 1914, resulted from a mixture of ardent love for mothers at the end of a period of intense maternalism, and the machinations of florists, who knew a good thing when they saw one. Indeed, the leading emotional advocate of Mother's Day, Anna Jarvis of Philadelphia, had by 1923 protested against the holiday: "This is not what I intended, I wanted it to be a day of sentiment, not profit."

Consumerism began to affect courtship. The idea of bringing simple gifts as part of courting was not new, but after 1910, again with the United States in the lead, young couples began to shift from conventional courtship to a new practice called dating. There were several differences between the forms, but one key distinction was that dating involved mixing some level of romance with attendance at a consumerist leisure event, such as a movie. And the romantic potential began to be evaluated in part by consumer standards: was the male providing enough? Was the female willing to reward consumer outlay by some favors in turn?

Consumerism also influenced divorce. Many couples began to quarrel over deficiencies in living standards: wives blamed husbands for not earning enough not simply for survival, but for consumer gains, and husbands attacked wives for shopping inadequacies. "You don't know enough to buy your own clothes," one aggrieved husband charged in Los Angeles in 1882, while in another case the husband ruefully noted his "inability to support [his wife] in the manner she desired on my salary." Not only earning levels, but also disagreements about whether to indulge in consumerism rather than focus on more basic necessities provided new reasons for couples to split, particularly in the middle classes.

We have seen that consumerism began to mix with childrearing. Parents began to find it increasingly normal to deal with behavior problems through consumerist manipulation – and children clearly added consumerism to their own evaluations of their position in the family. The pattern showed in several ways. Advice manuals began to urge parents to use material goods to distract their children from fear or anger. Is a child afraid of a dark room or a stranger? Place a desired consumer object close to the source of fear, to lure the child in. Does a child resent a sibling? Buy him something to show your love. And from children: a growing recorded amount of what was now called sibling rivalry often involved resentment that a brother or sister got a new toy. The association of consumer goods with emotional development and guidance grew steadily stronger.

Consumerism even began to affect emotional life directly. Growing opposition to conventional levels of grief began to develop soon after 1900, and a key reason was that grief, by definition a sad emotion, contradicted the kind of pleasure-seeking that consumerism implied. And the signs of grief – the heavy mourning clothes and extended periods of withdrawal – did begin to decline because they did not comport with larger consumerist attitudes.

Not surprisingly, consumerist intensity measurably increased. At an extreme, consumerist thefts now took on the quality of diseased compulsion. The newcomer was kleptomania, which involved thefts from department stores by (mainly) middle-class women who could in fact have paid for the goods they took. This was different in several ways from the consumerist theft patterns of the earlier, eighteenth-century phase, and above all it indicated how much further the consumer appetite could go in deviant cases. The problem affected both sides of the Atlantic. A Frenchwoman talked of going into department stores in a "genuine state of joy," as if she were meeting a lover. Another noted that she got more pleasure from her thefts than "from the father of her children." Simply handling fabrics such as silk could give intense sensual pleasure. And the passion simply could not be controlled. A woman who stole some alpaca wool, worth 43 francs, admitted that "the idea of possessing it had dominated her to the point of subjugating her will and her reason." English and American authorities, both legal and medical, identified the same kind of diseased reactions from the 1870s onward. The cases were atypical, prompted by mental illness of some sort, but the deviance did suggest how far consumerism could reach into personal life.

Causes revisited

Why did consumerism escalate so widely in this period? Some of the issues are familiar by now. A key factor involved changes in methods of production and distribution. European and American manufacturers were now capable of expanding their output to the point that selling it became an increasing problem. Mounting international competition and periodic economic recessions – a bad one hit in the 1870s, for example – drove this point home. Small wonder that there was growing pressure to make people believe they must buy a growing array of goods. The range of goods themselves expanded, as we have seen, which could help explain new levels of desire. And new technologies, for example in printing or otherwise conveying visually-dramatic advertising, amplified this kind of inducement. Part of the new consumerism resulted from new economic issues and technical means. Even kleptomania followed in part from the unprecedented existence of department stores, where the method of displaying goods facilitated theft and deliberately inflamed desire.

As before, the manipulation and apparatus of consumerism were not the whole story. By this point in Western history, a second set of factors resulted simply from consumerism's increasing familiarity. Many people now assumed that consumerist responses were appropriate, simply because the necessary ideas and behaviors had been around so long. This showed clearly, for example, in the increasing parental reliance on buying goods to help deal with their children. Because adults indulged in acquisition so often, there was only slight hesitation in coming to assume that children should do so. And of course the more consumer expectations were planted in childhood, the fuller their expression once adulthood loomed. Consumerism, in other words, was by this point feeding itself.

Many historians have also focussed on a third set of factors, which involves looking at new levels of consumerism as compensations for problems in other aspects of life. A set of causes involved in the first stage of consumerism, in other words, had some new counterparts by the late nineteenth century.

Three scenarios were involved. The first embraced workers, including (particularly in the United States) many immigrants. The unpleasantness of much industrial work had long been recognized. Gradually, some of the workers involved decided that, while the unpleasantness could not be reversed directly, it could be mitigated if labor could bid for a better life off the job. Work became less a goal in itself than an instrument for other gains. This instrumentalist approach first emerged among segments of British labor in the 1850s. It showed particularly in demands for higher wages, to compensate for work burdens, though reductions of hours could involve the instrumentalist approach as well. Goals of this sort readily translated into consumerist interests: for how was a better life off the job to be defined, how were the higher wages and shorter hours to be used, if not in new acquisitions or consumerist leisure? Obviously, workers did gradually win the kinds of resources that would permit more consumerism – here was a vital precondition for the whole phenomenon, however, not only resources but also new motives were involved.

Something of the same pattern occurred in the middle classes. By the late nineteenth century, many businessmen and professionals such as lawyers could no longer aspire to run their own operations, in the classic entrepreneurial fashion. Rather, they worked for large firms, serving as middle managers in corporations. These jobs might involve acceptable pay, but they were not as intrinsically satisfying, because of the need to work under the direction of other people. So middle-class men needed other outlets to demonstrate success and seek satisfaction, and this made consumerism more palatable. Even so, historians have demonstrated, intensification proceeded cautiously. The middle classes found it difficult to admit a candid new commitment to pleasure seeking. But they could justify leisure, including vacations, that was touted in terms of enhancing the capacity to work. They could buy products that would improve health. They could indulge in acquisitions with a family orientation. These targets easily led to an escalation of consumerism more generally, in a setting in which older satisfactions were becoming more elusive.

A growing new segment of the middle class needed consumer outlets even more directly. Lower-middle-class secretaries, sales personnel, telephone operators and others earned relatively low pay in jobs that were not working class, but involved a great deal of routine. Small wonder that lower-middle-class people were often at the forefront of new consumer interests. In Germany, for example, during the first decades of the twentieth century they led in cigarette smoking, in movie going, and in the purchase of radios. These were not items of great expense, but they did allow a sense of pleasure and identity – and the white-collar group definitely surpassed the working class, even at comparable levels of pay, in their pursuit.

Finally, there were women, particularly middle-class women. Resources increased for this group too, both because of a general if gradual increase in prosperity and because many women in this class now worked for a time before marriage, thus gaining direct access to money and some experience with new levels of consumption. But few women committed to work all of their life, because standards of respectability still argued against this. Women were, however, increasingly well educated. Their birth rates were dropping rapidly, and children spent growing amounts of time in school. These women were by no means idle, but they might well face new problems finding meaningful focus. Enter consumerism, once again, as a means of countering new problems with identity and providing not only new (if sometimes superficial) satisfaction, but also new meaning as well. Women served as the family's chief consumer agent in any event, in the industrial urban economy in which most men worked outside the home. It was not surprising that this specialization extended to growing engagement with shopping and with acquisition, though as we have seen women could also serve as family gatekeepers against excessive consumerism.

The causes of the full flowering of consumerism in the transatlantic world thus involved the new economic means and techniques of growing corporations; the habituation to consumerism itself, which fostered additional outpouring; and a set of new problems with other goals in life, associated both with work and with homemaking, which pushed consumerism as a surrogate compensation.

Additional issues

Consumerism around the turn of the twentieth century continued to involve a number of interesting issues. The old tension between comfort and elegance was redefined. Increasingly, though still in varying degrees, people now opted for comfort. Furniture became more fully upholstered, requiring less rigid posture. Clothing loosened, in part to permit more physical activity. There was even an inconclusive battle over women's corsets, held by some to be unhealthy as well as unpleasantly tight, by others as essential to preserve an appropriate figure. We will see that comfort did not always prevail, for example, stylish women's shoes often became less comfortable, but consumerism now encouraged at least an air of relaxation.

Gender was another issue. There is no question that women were particularly associated with this new phase of consumerism. They were the most visible shoppers, at an extreme the characteristic kleptomaniacs. Many critics of consumerism focussed on this gender angle, blaming stores and advertisers for picking on the weaker sex and blasting women for being so vulnerable. Gender wars occurred not only in the press, but, as we have seen, in individual families. Men were also consumerists. They almost certainly spent more on consumer goods than women did, and certainly they controlled more of the resources, but they did consume differently. They may have, on average, taken less pleasure in shopping, and they devoted less time to it. A 1920 study showed that they moved through department stores much faster than women did (and they disliked shopping where women congregated). They actually spent more on clothes. They certainly dominated the consumerist leisure field. They participated in large numbers of clubs and lodges (varying of course by social class, but with widespread involvement) that bought items such as billiard tables and drinking equipment. Many male groups had special uniforms and other fancy goods for display: an American lodge called the Pythians thus in 1887 required a "black silk folding chapeau trimmed with two black ostrich plumes . . . a gold tassel on each peak" and so on. Advertisers appealed to men as well as women, though using different outlets such as hunting and outdoor magazines. Overall, consumerism was not gender specific; it embraced both sexes, with fervor. But there are questions about why men and women had somewhat different styles and also why men chose to use consumerism as a basis for attack against women.

Another important set of questions involves consumerism's extent in Western life by the early twentieth century. We have seen how it gained ground in family relationships and in emotions. Did it even more basically color the ways people thought about the world around them? A number of cultural analysts refer to an increasing *commodification* in popular outlook, through which even phenomena outside the consumerist orbit would be thought of in consumerist terms. An example might be the female body. Women were increasingly featured in advertisements and of course, for some consumers, in pornography. They were encouraged not only to be fashionable, but also to smell good and, after 1900, to shave legs and underarms as part of escalating beauty standards. Were their bodies seen by men, and possibly by women themselves, as commodities, to be evaluated in some of the same ways that consumer goods were assessed?

A final issue involves the uses of consumerism in protest, where developments in the West would ultimately be matched by innovations elsewhere. Obviously, once a society commits to significant new consumer expenses, it also has a new weapon: withholding those commitments, to protest some social wrong. Not surprisingly, some use of consumer boycotts began early, as in Britain's American colonies. American revolutionaries, dumping British tea in Boston, were saying that reform was more important than regular tea drinking. Anti-slavery movements, particularly in Britain, discussed boycotting products (particularly cotton) that came from slave labor. Boycotting picked up in the acceleration of consumerism after the late nineteenth century. A number of boycotts were directed against products made by sweatshop labor. During the 1920s and 1930s, African Americans, in cities such as Baltimore, used boycotts to protest discrimination in employment and in urban facilities. Boycotts reveal the growing economic and political importance of consumerism – otherwise, withdrawal of purchasing would have had no impact – but also the willingness of key groups periodically to put other goals first. Some boycotts won reforms, others failed – sometimes because not enough people were willing to change their consumer behaviors. An interesting twist on boycotts occurred in the United States in the 1930s. To protest Japanese invasion of China, groups urged a boycott of silk. Here, however, instead of urging sacrifice, promoters argued that other products were just as stylish: one could protest without abandoning consumerism. This may have been yet another indication of the intensification of the whole phenomenon.

Advancing consumerism raises some tough analytical questions. It clearly continued to embrace important tensions, between stylishness and comfort; or male and female; or enjoyment versus protest. And as we will see in the following chapter, it also provoked profound uneasiness. Never before had so many people spent so much time working at consuming. Small wonder that consumerism affected views of the world as well as daily life, or that it prompted new guilts and anxieties.

International outreach

The escalation of Western consumerism inevitably spilled over into the wider world. Commercial forces pushing consumerism at home could hardly avoid the temptation to seek buyers elsewhere. Europeans and Americans now found consumerism so natural that they took it with them virtually anywhere they went; even missionaries, deeply devoted to the cause of the Christian God, brought the apparatus of consumption with them in many ways. Diplomatic representatives imported the new spectator sports: the first soccer club in Argentina was formed by British residents in 1867, leading to a first national league of Argentine teams by the 1890s. American and European movies were being shown in Africa and Latin America by 1900. Hollywood companies opened international branches quickly. Universal Studios had 20 such outlets by 1918, in countries such as Indonesia, Japan, India, and Singapore. By the early 1920s American films controlled 95 percent of the Australian market. We will turn to the larger international impact in Part II, but it is important to note how its expansion dovetailed with its unprecedented triumph within the Western world.

Further reading

Elaine Abelson, *When Ladies Go A-thieving: Middle-class Shoplifters in the Victorian Department Store* (New York: Oxford University Press, 1989); Susan Porter Benson, *Counter Cultures: Saleswomen, Managers, and Customers in American Department Stores, 1890–1940* (Urbana: University of Illinois Press, 1986); John Benson, *The Rise of Consumer Society in Britain, 1880–1980* (New York: Longman, 1994); Lizabeth Cohen, *Making a New Deal: Industrial Workers in Chicago, 1919–1939* (New York: Cambridge University Press, 1990); Richard W. Fox and Jackson Lears, eds, *The Culture of Consumption: Critical Essays in American History, 1880–1980* (New York: Pantheon Books, 1983); Allen Guttman, *Sports Spectators* (New York: Columbia University Press, 1986); Eva Illouz, *Consuming the Romantic Utopia: Love and the Cultural Contradictions of Capitalism* (Berkeley, CA: University of California Press, 1997); Sut Jhally, *The Codes of Advertising: Fetishism and the Political Economy of Meaning in the Consumer Society* (New York; London: Routledge, 1990); Alan Kidd and David Nicholls, eds, *Gender, Civic Culture and Consumerism: Middle-Class Identity in Britain 1800–1940* (New York: St. Martin's Press, 1999); Roland Marchand, *Advertising the American Dream* (Berkeley, CA: University of California Press, 1985); Michael Miller, *The Bon Marché: Bourgeois Culture and the Department Store, 1869–1920* (Princeton, NJ:

Princeton University Press, 1981); Stephen Nissenbaum, *The Battle for Christmas* (New York: Vintage Books, 1996); Benjamin Rader, *Baseball: a History of America's Game* (Urbana, IL: University of Illinois Press, 1992); Charles Rearick, *Pleasures of the Belle Epoque: Entertainment and Festivity in Turn-of-the Century France* (New Haven, CT: Yale University Press, 1985); Roy Rosenzweig, *Eight Hours for What we Will: Workers and Leisure in an Industrial City, 1870–1920* (New York: Cambridge University Press, 1985); Peter N. Stearns, *Battleground of Desire: the Struggle for Self-control in Modern America* (New York: New York University Press, 1999); Vincent Vinikas, *Soft Soap, Hard Sell: American Hygiene in an Age of Advertisement* (Ames, IA: Iowa State University Press, 1992); John K. Walton, T*he Blackpool Landlady: a Social History* (Manchester: Manchester University Press, 1978); Rosalind Williams, *Dream Worlds: Mass Consumption in Late Nineteenth Century France* (Berkeley, CA: University of California Press, 1982). See also L. Black and H. Pemberton, eds, *An Affluent Society? Britain's Post War "Gold Age" Revisited* (London: Ashgate, 2004); and Lisa Tiersten, *Marianne in the Market: Envisioning Consumer Society in Fin-de-siecle France* (Berkeley, CA: University of California Press, 2001).

Chapter 6

The dark side of Western consumerism

Thus far the story of consumerism may seem like a record of steady advance (whether you judge this a good thing or not). Except for the lull in the early nineteenth century, and apart from briefer though sometimes severe interruptions caused by economic recession or war, consumerism has seemed to gain ground with every passing decade. Yet consumerism also prompted doubts in every phase. These emerged by the later eighteenth and early nineteenth centuries, and (not surprisingly) an even greater array greeted the expansion of consumerism around 1900. This chapter deals with the critics of consumerism, important in Western society as a counterpoint to the larger development. Even more, it tackles some of the wider guilts these critics could reflect and encourage.

Consumerism has always been hard to protest against. Its manifestations are amorphous. Many people seemed to such as some features of consumerism from the first, even if they hesitated about the larger phenomenon. How can the idea of a better material life be attacked? What's wrong with consumerist leisure forms that almost everyone seems to enjoy? Individual critics of consumerism can easily sound like elitist grumps.

Collective action against consumerism has proved even more difficult, at least in the Western world. Before modern times, people often protested high prices, particularly of basic necessities such as bread; this was a consumer, but not a consumerist protest. Some bread riots continued in the nineteenth and twentieth centuries. By this point, however, popular protest most commonly seized on issues at work or in politics: strikes and protest voting represented these grievances. Of course consumer anxieties might play into these protests, when people thought they lacked enough money to meet their expectations. But consumerism was not the target. Very occasionally, as before the American Revolution, boycotts used consumerism as a more direct vehicle, withdrawing purchases to protest some other target. Consumer boycotts have historically been hard to pull off, because they depend on an elusive loyalty; many people break the boycott precisely because they yearn to buy. But even boycotts do not call consumerism per se into question. Only in the twentieth century, in fact, do mass protests against consumerism emerge, and then most commonly outside the West.

But difficulties and absence of clear collective protest should not suggest that consumerism was home free in the modern West. A host of groups did include attacks on consumerism at least as part of other grievances. Still more important, though harder to pin down, many ordinary individuals worried about their own engagement in consumerism, seeking to find some outlet for real guilt about indulgence even as they continued to indulge.

This chapter deals with these undercurrents to modern consumerism, which altered life and outlook even as consumerism worked its own magic. It also shows how different cultures within the transatlantic orbit generated somewhat different reactions. Consumerism was not monolithic, and reactions to it varied as well. This was a story that would be played out in a still larger framework as the twentieth century advanced and the phenomenon took hold worldwide.

Hostility to consumerism obviously suggests how new modern consumerism was, how many concerns it could raise. Attacks on consumerism were themselves an important part of modern history, first in Western society, then more generally. Accommodations between critique and advance help explain why specific consumer patterns emerged as they did, and why some societies have experienced fuller consumerist development than others. Even within the West, the more modest nature of anti-consumerist movements in the United States and Britain contrast with patterns on the European continent.

Early comment

Initial reactions to consumerism in the first, eighteenth-century phase, typically picked up traditional Christian moral themes, in attacks on greed and gluttony and about pursuing false gods. Because consumerism was so new, more specific themes did not initially emerge. Criticism of the disruption of proper social hierarchy, with lower classes taking on life styles appropriately confined to their social superiors, allowed expression of other concerns. By the early nineteenth century, this commentary was supplemented by frequent laments about how poor people were driving themselves deeper into poverty by buying things they did not need. This argument could also be applied to immigrants and African Americans, in the United States, and to women.

Moralists were certainly aware of the scope and danger of change. As early as 1711, an English writer, John Dennis, deemed "Luxury" the "spreading Contagion which is the greatest Corruption of Publick Manners and the greatest Extinguisher of Publick Spirit." A great deal of attention was devoted to what critics claimed was a growing level of illness associated with overindulgence. There were two points here. In the first place, the word consumption itself at this point had two meanings: the buying of goods, but also respiratory disease including tuberculosis. In this latter sense, it was possible to die of consumption. Some writers deliberately punned on the double meaning as a way of attacking consumerism: "Consumption may be regarded as a vast pit-fall, situated on the high road of life, which we have not sense enough of our common interest to agree to fill up, or fence round." A second way to attack consumerism through illness was to focus on diseases of the stomach, or appetite, where overindulgence could literally affect the body. Many eighteenth-century critics in England thus urged the importance of plain food, using this as a symbol of self-restraint more generally.

Sickness became associated, in this early commentary, with growing ease and city ways, a linkage that would persist into later periods. The commentator who argued that "consumption prevails more in England than in any other part of the world" was thus explicitly claiming that there were more indulgence-related illnesses, but also sought to imply that England suffered generally from exceptionally high and harmful levels of consumerism.

Some critics took this point further, arguing that societies as well as individuals might suffer from overindulgence. An eighteenth-century English comment contrasted desirable simplicity with the kind of luxury that would drive a nation into decline. He worried about groups grown "luxurious and wanton" and also picked up another common theme, anti-foreignness, in warning against "frequent commerce with other nations."

Not surprisingly, criticisms of this sort arose in the United States by the early nineteenth century. Previously, as we have seen, consumerism could be attacked as foreign – British, and then French; and it could be subjected to the baleful comments by Protestant preachers attacking distractions from awareness of mortal sin and from devotion to spiritual goals. These attacks, first surfacing in the later eighteenth century, continued into the 1850s. A new element arose in the 1830s, with a series of purification movements directed against the twin evils of commercialism and sexuality. Particularly interesting and influential was the campaign of Sylvester Graham, in the 1840s, to wean Americans from the excesses of a market society. His focus was not consumerism alone, but also the broader engagement with commercial mechanisms and what he saw as undue sexuality. His remedy, however, was revealing, as he urged pure food and plain diets, as against standard commercial products and also excessive fats. Vegetarianism, concentrated on healthy grains such as those contained in his new graham cracker, would prevent over stimulation both in the sexual and the consumer arenas. Graham's message of simple foods, temperance and chastity won many converts for a time, particularly among young, urban men. And there were other crusaders for pure food products, including Kellogg, as part of the same general reaction to an increasingly commercial economy. The linkage between restraint of consumerism and both moral and physical health was an urgent one.

Phase II: new critical approaches

The escalation of consumerism in the second phase, from the late nineteenth into the early twentieth centuries, brought a renewed round of reaction, which proved to be far broader, and less dependent on purely traditional morality, than the initial set. Clearly, consumerism's earlier development had not produced enough concurrence to prevent a new round of attack. And, on the whole, the attacks were wider ranging than before, in terms of argument and audience alike. Moralistic comment continued, to be sure. Children's reading matter in the United States and England, for example, maintained traditional attacks on envy, in favor of being resigned to one's lot in life and taking pleasure in God, until about 1920. A typical poem, in a literature book for children, thus intoned:

> Let us work! We only ask
> Reward proportioned to our task;
> We have no quarrel with the great
> No feud with rank – with mill or bank.

Another earlier theme extended attacks on people who consumed at the expense of appropriate saving or class distinctions. Workers could still be blasted for delighting in items they could not really afford. Women came in for more adverse comment than ever before. Well into the twentieth century, blasts against women's weakness and irrationality focussed heavily on their responsibility for growing consumerism. In France, novelist Emile Zola wrote a whole book about department stores and their lures to flighty, frivolous women (*The Ladies' Paradise*). Zola could not decide who were more at fault, the storeowners for setting out temptations or women for being so empty-headed as to succumb. Doctors' discovery of kleptomania was widely publicized, on both sides of the Atlantic, occasioning another round of attacks on women for being such ready victims.

But there were even newer themes in the attacks on the consumer advance that were also important. Blasts at consumerism were much more politicized in this period, and here several groups and targets might be involved. In Europe, a new kind of anti-Semitism developed in the final decades of the nineteenth century. Jews were attacked for many things, but their role as owners of department stores loomed large in the new movement. This was in part an expression of dismay by shopkeepers in countries such as France and Germany about new levels of competition. But some slaps at consumerism were involved as well, as Jewish owners could be seen as provoking the appetites of otherwise reasonable Christians.

By the 1920s, Nazism, in part an extension of the earlier anti-Semitism, also harbored a pronounced anti-consumerist element. Nazis wanted people to value the state, the race and the leader, not to be distracted by individual consumerist goals. They specifically attacked fashion, in the name of more traditional costumes – such as the flowered skirts and aprons for women known in Austria and southern Germany as *dirndls*. All sort of motives flowed into Nazism of course, of which uneasiness with consumerism was not a trivial component.

Socialists also attacked consumerism, though there were ambiguities here. Socialist leaders were obviously hostile to capitalism, and therefore to the inequalities of consumerism under capitalism. Many hoped for a purified, moral working class that would rise above consumer lures. Some actually repeated a certain element of the bourgeois critique about frivolous spending. Many hoped that workers could be taught to value good literature rather than consumerist trash. But the fact was that most workers seemed to prefer the trash. Their quarrel with capitalism involved poor working conditions and inadequate wages, more than consumerism. So over time, socialist attacks on shallow consumerism tended to decline in favor of vigorous advocacy of greater equality. In the 1930s, even the French communist movement would join in encouraging young workers to take an interest in fashion and cosmetics, as part of enticing more youth into communist ranks.

Along with conservative anti-Semites and a number of labor leaders, many intellectuals also picked on consumerism. Motives were mixed: some attacked shallowness and misplaced values, while others, blasting debased mass taste, were also concerned about the destruction of conventional social hierarchy. The opening of giant department stores in German cities in the 1890s triggered sweeping commentary. Particular attention focussed on the moral decline of the middle class, as it became increasingly involved with consumerism. Thomas Mann's classic *Buddenbrooks*, the most famous German novel of the period, traced a middle-class dynasty brought low by loss of self-restraint amid increasingly posh surroundings. The family ends with a prodigal son who turns from simplicity to dandyism and dies, appropriately enough, of consumption (again, the play on words). Sociologists also attacked the lack of taste and character involved in vulgar displays of wealth. Historians demonstrated that whole societies declined when people turned from virtue to a devotion to material affluence; the fall of Rome was frequently invoked. Another common criticism, recalling the blasts against women, held the growth of consumerism to be a sign of effeminacy in German culture. Finally, consumerism was seen as foreign; if not Jewish, at least French: as one writer put it, "the department store has nothing to do with German culture." Others lamented the "thoughtless import of foreign fashions . . . we see our German women squeezed into French fashion clothing which was cut for the bodies of a differently built race."

These attacks were not without response. Other German writers praised the growth of prosperity and argued that lower-class tastes were improved through contact with better styles and department stores. On the nationalist front, some urged that German fashions be sold worldwide, establishing a lead in global consumerism while doing away with unnecessary foreign influence at home. But debate continued, as many German intellectuals, and their middle-class and aristocratic audience clearly felt uncomfortable with the growing consumerism around them and what it implied for the future of their society.

Nor were Germans alone in the discussion. In the United States, economist Thorstein Veblen wrote a widely-read study of the unnecessary luxury of upper-class business magnates, coining the term "conspicuous consumption" to highlight spending that merely served as show, meeting neither real needs nor genuine aesthetic standards. Veblen was not calling ordinary consumerism into question, but some of his commentary could be more widely applied.

Critique did not end with World War I. The 1920s saw renewed sneers against women, Jews, capitalists, and the deteriorating standards of mass society coming again from a variety of sources, from fascism through traditionalist intellectuals to communism. This was of course the period when Nazis touted devotion to leader and nation over corrupting consumer influences. Nazi leaders (who themselves indulged in various consumer pleasures, including fashion shows) obviously hoped to channel resources toward military preparation, but they also professed to prefer peasant simplicity on moral and racial grounds.

And a new element was now added in: anti-Americanism. Reacting to growing United States influence, attacks on the foreign qualities of consumerism in Europe increasingly focussed on American extensions, both because American stores and standards were gaining ground abroad and because the United States could serve as a symbol of consumerism more generally, a target for all that was disliked in modern consumer life. The Dutch historian Johan Huizinga thus wrote of a visit to the United States: "Your instruments of civilization and progress . . . only make us nostalgic for what is old and quaint, and sometimes your life seems hardly to be worth living." More abruptly, the German Oswald Spengler simply opined, "Life in America is exclusively economic in structure and lacks depth." French writer Georges Duhamel held American materialism up as a beacon of mediocrity that threatened to eclipse French civilization, imposing worthless "needs and appetites" on humanity at large. Anti-American anti-consumerism became something of a national hobby in France. During the 1930s debate focussed on whether cheap-goods outlets such as Woolworths, called dime stores in the United States, should be copied in France. Opponents claimed that dime stores debased women and workers by inducing them to spend heedlessly. They argued that real Frenchness was hostile to mass consumerism on grounds of inherent French taste and quality. The French parliament, in 1936, banned American-style outlets for a year on the grounds that they "fooled" their customers and constituted a foreign intrusion against the virtues of French style. The practical result was at most a compromise: new outlets did spread, offering cheap goods in chain stores such as Monoprix, but with some greater effort to offer a veneer of craftsmanship. Debate resumed after World War II, when American consumer influence expanded even further; it was a French intellectual who coined the clever critical phrase to describe American cultural control, "cocacolonisation."

The fascist alternative

Particularly during the decades between the wars, hostility to consumerism was far more than talk and scapegoating: it led to significant legislation, as in the French moves against American-style stores. But the most important efforts to beat back consumerism formed part of the fascist movement in Italy and Germany, where developments occurred that resembled the anti-consumerist backlash that would emerge in other parts of the world such as Japan.

Fascist and Nazi leaders obviously tried to appeal to a public concern about consumer values and foreign influences. To artisans, for example, they evoked a world that would return to craft production and artistic values, as opposed to the mass taste exemplified by department stores (which, the Nazis would add, were also Jewish owned). Recommendations that women return to the home, have children, and wear traditional peasant dress countered the rapid advance of women in public consumerism, for example in the Germany of the 1920s. Some of these attacks were largely rhetorical: fascists and Nazis, in power, did not really restore an artisanal economy, for they needed industrial muscle to advance their plans for war. Certain consumer staples continued to gain under fascism and Nazism – including the purchase of Coca-Cola, that quintessential American product.

Basic fascist goals, however, were anti-consumerist. For fascist leaders, modern society had become too disunited and individualistic. Consumerism was a fundamental part of modern degeneracy. Great emphasis, both in fascist Italy and Nazi Germany, was placed on returning to national traditions, abandoning pernicious foreign styles. People should return to group loyalties, under a powerful Leader. Consumerism, in this vision, should be replaced by standardized uniforms – the black and brown shirts of the fascist legions. Young people should learn group discipline in appropriate youth groups, rather than exploring imported musical styles or personalized fashions. Workers should be content with a fairly low wage, spiced by opportunities to take vacations in standardized, factory-like resorts, such as the huge complex Hitler built at Rostock, on the Baltic Sea. The Nazis indeed organized an elaborate Strength through Joy movement, designed to immerse ordinary people in nature hikes and heart-stirring collective rallies, as an alternative to any significant consumerist gains. Even earlier, in fascist Italy during the 1920s, Mussolini's regime had organized after-work (*dopolavoro*) programs designed to wean workers (carefully including women) from both socialism and consumerism; the emphasis, again, was on coordination and group loyalty, highlighted by common, government-sponsored uniforms. On a more prosaic basis, both fascist and Nazi leaders urged high personal savings, which obviously could support public investment and mitigate low wages. And ultimately, of course, the purpose of fascist society was war, not consumerism. The battle against consumerism entered the mainstream of German and Italian history for two crucial decades.

American guilt: a special case?

Explicit attacks on consumerism became more common in Western Europe than in the United States, during the decades after 1900. Obviously, nothing like a fascist attack on consumerism developed across the waters. One difference is immediately obvious: anti-Americanism was irrelevant within the United States, and there was no comparable foreign symbol as a critical target against consumerism. Americans had earlier condemned Britain or France as sources of undesirable luxury and softness, but by 1900 the American lead in consumerism outweighed importation. If consumerism was a fault, it was now a domestic fault. It was now the West Europeans who could claim foreign corruption, however unfairly.

This did not mean that Americans failed to worry about consumerism. We will see that they worried quite a bit, even as they participated, but the more common villains were less available, even aside from the anti-foreign angle. For example: turn-of-the-century Americans were often anti-Semitic, but their anti-Semitism was less extreme than that which developed among some Europeans, and it did not focus on Jews as consumer leaders; at most, Jewish bad taste and garishness might be a small part of this particular racial bias. The more virulent kinds of American racism did not release consumerist anxiety. Consumerism did not figure among the leading African American faults, in the racist vision. Even the Ku Klux Klan, which revived in the 1920s to attack both racial minorities and some of the flaws of modern life, did not seize on consumerism with any coherence. It was true that Americans recurrently attacked African Americans for wearing unduly flashy clothes or buying expensive cars. As in European attacks on the working class, this reflected a sense that certain groups did not "deserve" showy consumerism and that they were wasting their money and displaying a lack of good character and restraint. These complaints could even feed racial rioting, as when Americans in World War II attacked "zoot-suited" African Americans (and Mexican Americans) who seemed to be enjoying consumer pleasures while white men served in the military. But this racist component was not an attack on consumerism per se, but a focus on a suspect racial group. It may have released various tensions, but not the anxieties that consumerism itself provoked.

Nor was American socialism well enough developed to serve as a major outlet for critiques of consumerism. Here was another contrast with Europe, where socialist movements gained ground steadily. American trade unionism was better developed, but for the most part trade union attacks either ignored consumerism, in their focus on working conditions, or sought better wages that would allow fuller worker participation. Even attacks on women were milder in the United States. American commentary on kleptomania might note that some ladies had a "mania for pretty things," but the scathing commentary on female frivolity and vulnerability so common in countries such as France was largely missing. And while some American intellectuals worried about mass taste, their concerns were far less frenzied than those of their European counterparts.

There were two related reasons for the softer tone of American reactions. First, the nation prided itself on the absence of political extremes, which worked against fervent rightwing anti-Semitism or leftwing socialism or communism. Second, lacking traditional social hierarchy and the same hallowed position for intellectuals that Europe could offer, Americans found it more difficult to develop a clear and durable basis for anti-consumerist critiques. There was no well-established aristocratic taste to refer to. It was harder for intellectuals to excoriate mass taste without seeming like un-democratic, irrelevant snobs.

On the surface, then, consumerism had smoother sailing in the United States than in Western Europe, once it reached the second, turn-of-the-century phase. The nation's huge market, its outpouring of products, led to the seeming triumph of consumer values that European observers often feared.

Surfaces can be deceiving. American anxieties about consumerism existed, but they had to be sought with greater subtlety. We have already seen in Chapter 5 how proponents of consumerism had to invoke sounder values, even in the United States, to draw middle-class favor. Crass appeals were often masked by references to health or family, which suggests that even Americans might grow uncomfortable with unmitigated materialism. Even without a tradition of aristocratic taste, there were bases for collective comment. Religion of course was one, and while its service had been modified by the adjustments of mainstream Protestantism, Americans could still wonder about consumer values in relation to higher, spiritual goals. Discomfort with the commercialization of Christmas provided a prosaic but regular focus for some of these comparisons. Newer movements picked up other uneasiness. By the early twentieth century some Americans were swept up by concerns about the environment, which could offer an alternative to consumerist priorities. The middle and upper class also developed a clear sense of high-brow culture – opera, symphonies, and Shakespearean plays – which it newly contrasted with mass taste. Even more broadly, distrust of city life and urban values (even by Americans who did not really want to live outside the city) could include some hesitations about consumerist gains.

Americans also expressed concerns about consumerism in terms of personal ethics. The same decades that saw the triumph of American consumer values and the onset of international leadership in consumer institutions, saw several new counterthrusts in the name of personal discipline. Temperance was one. Attacks on excessive consumption of alcohol had begun earlier in American history, but it was in the first part of the twentieth century that they won through in the form of Prohibition. Americans might be indulgent in some respects, but they would also vote for movements that pulled them back in others. Efforts to outlaw cigarette smoking surfaced at the same time. Both these movements dwindled by the 1930s, of course, but they served as important moralistic vehicles for a time.

Americans also worried about commercial films and other consumer out-croppings such as comic books. Even as the nation led the world in consumer leisure, moralists attacked open sexuality or media violence. Divisions among groups, for example between more and less religious observers, but also tensions within individuals, generated recurrent anxiety.

A less political but vigorous crusade for better posture was another explicit reaction to advanced consumerism. Here too, standards had been set earlier, but in the nineteenth century few groups worried greatly about posture training. The situation changed by 1900. Various reformers began to mount posture training programs for schools. A National Posture League formed. Colleges starting testing students for posture, instituting remedial courses for those who failed. Parents were urged to discipline their children's posture, and kits were available to provide appropriate standards. Two concerns prompted the program, both related to consumerism. First, posture advo-cates noted the growing reliance on comfort, in furnishings and clothing; posture now had to be taught, because clothing and chairs did not provide automatic support. Second, posture became an emblem of the growing soft-ness and temptation of life in consumer society. Too much ease might undermine moral fiber, and posture was a symbol of rigorous response.

Over time, by the 1940s and 1950s, the posture crusade receded, but the idea of moral antidote did not. Dieting and attacking weight centered another campaign for self-criticism and discipline clearly related to consumerism, and the movement took on particular moral overtones in the United States. Efforts to stay thin or become more slender began to develop in the 1890s, and accelerated fairly steadily from that point onward. Reasons included increasingly abundant food and increasingly sedentary jobs, along with changes in disease patterns that countered more traditional beliefs that plumpness was a sign of health, but many diet gurus also argued that keeping weight off signaled strength of character in an indulgent consumer society. Foods had already been identified as a key consumer symbol. What changed was the urgency and wide appeal of pleas for restraint in eating.

Fat became a clear sign of laziness and bad character. Doctors, urging weight loss, frequently commented more widely on the relationship between fat and "the changes in the mode of living that characterize present-day urban existence." Simon Patten, an economist who praised consumer progress in many respects, also urged control of "crude appetites," and the key was moderation in eating. Writing between 1895 and 1910, he repeatedly invoked the "steady improvement of appetite control." Increasingly, attacks on fat took on the characteristics of a moral crusade, particularly applicable to women but relevant to men as well.

The United States proved capable of generating additional campaigns to demonstrate moral control, in the cause of health but also to demonstrate good character in an age of abundance. Strongly moralistic attacks on smoking in the 1970s showed the eagerness with which many Americans could turn to new or renewed targets for abstinence, to show that they were not helpless victims of consumerism.

Conclusion: undercurrents of anxiety

The development and expansion of consumerism raised issues of personal goals and social purpose. At various times and places, many people expressed concern and many more felt it, however obscurely. People who cherished more traditional values, including religious values, could not help but feel some tension with advancing consumerism. Consumer society also raised other issues, about relationships among social groups and between genders, that could spur dismay. People who benefited from one phase of consumerism, such as shopkeepers, might suffer from a subsequent phase that featured other consumer apparatus such as department stores, and they would not be silent.

Like the development of consumer society itself, expressions of anxiety varied somewhat from one region to the next. The United States had produced fewer direct or political attacks on consumerism than other societies by 1900, but many Americans did generate a moral uneasiness that may have surpassed comparable developments in Western Europe. Certainly, all through the twentieth century, many Europeans found Americans' personal moralism distinctly odd. French doctors, to take one specific example, were just as eager to urge weight loss as their American counterparts, but they talked in terms of health and beauty alone, not morality; and they specifically condemned American tendencies to make overweight people feel they were deficient in character. In comparative terms, the United States by the 1900s had established both the most extensive consumer apparatus, and some of the most unabashed consumer interest, while also producing some distinctive signs of individual guilt and compensation. Even within the Western world, consumer societies and the responses they generated were not all the same.

Whether personal or political, attacks on consumerism rarely slowed the advance of consumer behavior in Western Europe or the United States. Only extreme situations, such as Nazism in Germany, where anti-consumerism was part of a larger political tide, saw significant modifications – and even here, Hitler catered to some consumer impulses. Simply put, in most situations, from the eighteenth century onward, the forces propelling consumerism were stronger than those opposing it in the Western world. Criticisms of other people's consumer behavior, relatedly, proved easier than criticisms of one's own. Yet the anxieties consumerism caused were part of real history as well, even if they were not triumphant. Individuals and groups had mixed feelings, even as they increasingly indulged. Consumer society, even in its Western birthplace, was inherently complex, precisely because it challenged widely accepted norms. Had the anxieties about consumerism disappeared in the Western world by the advent of the twenty-first century?

Certainly, the most explicit attacks on consumerism receded in Western society after World War II. The defeat of fascism discredited the most general effort to stem consumerism and replace it with a more military and collective identity. This did not mean, of course, that more diffuse guilt about consumerism ended, as we have seen in the American case; and there were new objections to consumerism as well, particularly from an environmental standpoint. Finally, particularly in Western Europe, some legacy may have persisted from the intense debate, between the world wars, about consumerism itself. While the fascist alternative was rejected, some Europeans still looked to definitions of life and economic activity that would not be consumerist alone.

This may help explain why, as we will discuss in Chapter 11, contemporary European consumerism has taken a somewhat different form from its American counterpart. Objections to consumerism played a major role in Western history, particularly in the early decades of the twentieth century; their impact is less obvious today, but it may still affect the context within which consumers operate.

Further reading

David Horowitz, *The Morality of Spending: Attitudes Toward the Consumer Society in America* (Chicago, IL: I.R. Dee, 1993); Rosalind Williams, *Dream Worlds: Mass Consumption in Late Nineteenth Century France* (Berkeley, CA: University of California Press, 1982); Peter N. Stearns, *Fat History: Bodies and Beauty in the Modern West* (New York: New York University Press, 1997); Bonnie Smith, *Ladies of the Leisure Class: The Bourgeoises of Northern France in the Nineteenth Century* (Princeton, NJ: Princeton University Press,

1981). On objections to consumerism, particularly between the world wars: Victoria de Grazia, *Culture of Consent: Mass Organization of Leisure in Fascist Italy* (New York: Cambridge University Press, 1981); Victoria de Grazia with Ellen Furlough, *The Sex of Things: Gender and Consumption in Historical Perspective* (Berkeley, CA: University of California Press, 1996); Martin Daunton and Matthew Hilton, *The Politics of Consumption: Material Culture and Citizenship in Europe and America* (New York: Berg Press, 2001); Matthew Hilton, *Consumerism in Twentieth-Century Britain* (New York: Cambridge University Press, 2003); and Gary Cross, *Time and Money: the Making of Consumer Culture* (London: Routledge, 1993).

Part II

Consumerism goes global

The elements of consumerism that had existed in pre-modern societies obviously had a global context. Pre-modern consumerism had developed more extensively in China and the Middle East than in Western Europe, before the modern centuries. It also depended heavily on international trade – for example, on Chinese silks. This section returns to world history, this time for modern consumerism.

Western consumerism had itself depended heavily on global context. It had been stimulated in part by access to new goods from other parts of the world: sugar, silk, Indian cotton. It depended also on the profits from world trade, including the slave trade, which had fed not only goods but money into Western Europe and North America. Additional production supplied Western consumerism by the nineteenth century: for example, production of Middle Eastern ("oriental") carpets accelerated rapidly to meet the demands of European and American households. But the full world history of modern consumerism also involves the spread of consumer styles and interests from the West to other places. Dissemination to the Americas was an early part of this process. Elements of consumerism – sometimes, to be sure, superficial elements – often formed part of initial reactions to new Western contacts – such was the case with Japan by the 1870s, for instance. The worldwide spread of modern consumerism, and limitations and special adaptations within this process, form the core of the chapters that follow.

Chapters in this section deal with the spread of modern consumerism to societies in Eastern Europe, Asia, Africa, and Latin America. The time period ranges from the early nineteenth century, when Western forms of consumerism first made serious contact with a wider orbit, to the later twentieth century.

Some of the reasons for the spread of consumerism are fairly obvious. As Western contacts proliferated through growing trade and colonialism, Western businessmen and diplomats themselves modeled aspects of consumerism to other peoples. They were not fully comfortable without at least elements of behaviors common back home. The spread of Western tourism, more recently, has had a similar impact. There was also the desire to sell or cajole: persuading other people to be open to new forms of consumerism brought the promise of larger markets for Western-made goods and for easier acceptance of colonial rule. Domestic components entered as well. Some societies already had certain elements of consumer interest – in varied and colorful clothing for example. China was a case in point here. Almost all societies relied on material distinctions as markers of social status, and consumerism might fit in here. And finally, consumerism could serve to cushion or legitimate other kinds of social and economic change, as had been the case in the West itself.

But consumerism did not spread evenly or uniformly. A combination of convergence and differentiation is crucial to the chapters that follow. Some societies were readier for consumerism than others, and variations of this sort raise obvious questions of causation. Different kinds of resistance developed as well, which can be compared additionally to reactions in the West itself. This section deals with a number of instances of consumerism, each with its own timing and flavor. While there is no effort to cover all major societies, the range of historical experiences will be clear.

Expanding global consumerism, in other words, had some common elements, including examples, products, and marketing methods spreading from the West. But outside influence was encountered in various ways. Prior traditions played a key role; not surprisingly, at least temporary resistance to consumerism was clearest in cases where a strong, preconsumerist ideology maintained vigorous hold. Economic circumstances also affected response: some societies remained poorer than others, some were more fully engulfed by a low-wage economy that featured production for a global market but few opportunities to share in this market as consumers. The chapters in this section invite careful comparative analysis.

The global extensions of consumerism involved aspects of what is sometimes called Westernization. Indeed, Western consumer forms may turn out to be the most successful Western influence in world history, more eagerly sought, for example, than political democracy, although a Westernization model risks implying undue homogeneity. Few societies embraced Western-style consumerism without some modifications, and a number held back altogether, at least for many decades, in the name of more traditional values or clearer identities. Modern consumerism, complex enough in its Western birthplace, added complexities as it widened.

The following chapters deal with the evolution of consumerism in Russia; in East Asia, with Chinese and Japanese comparisons; in Latin America; in Africa; and in the Middle East. There is a rough chronology here. Russia, close to the West geographically and culturally, picked up consumer elements fairly early. East Asia began to grapple seriously during the final third of the nineteenth century. Latin America and Africa, though interestingly distinct, saw an acceleration of interest from the 1920s onward –

at a time when several societies, in Asia and parts of Europe, were actually reconsidering the consumerist thrust. The Middle East encountered elements of modern consumerism earlier than this, though here too the 1920s saw intensification; but a particularly dramatic set of trends and conflicts emerged after the 1970s. The five major cases do not, of course, exhaust the world's regions, but they provide ample evidence of the common pressures and motives, and also the distinctive kinds of reception and resistance, that modern consumerism involved as it gained the world stage.

Consumerism in all these cases was heavily foreign, a clear import, even as it appealed to both new and traditional interests. Foreignness, in turn, generated three reactions. The first involved the appeal of the strange and, apparently, the modern; consumerism meant more than acquisition, it meant association with a larger set of images. But second, foreignness prompted resistance, in the name of customary but also newer national identities. Elements of this had colored even the reception of consumerism in the United States and Europe, but elsewhere the tide ran stronger. Third, foreignness did not have to be eternal. By experience, and by combining with local styles and values, consumerism could be appropriated, becoming as "natural" as it was in the West.

There was no single pattern, which is why comparison is so vital. The three reactions to foreignness could combine in quite varied ways. Different modes of encounter with the West, different political structures and experiences, colored consumerism. But the most important factor was history itself, as consumerism had to interact with distinctive regional cultures and interests.

Chapter 7

Consumerism in Russia

Russia's experience with consumerism has been complex and revealing. The country was closely linked to Western culture before consumerism took full hold elsewhere in Europe. The links have consistently tempted Russians of various sorts to embrace consumerism as a sign of civilization and the measure of a good life. But Russia was also traditionally highly rural and religious. By 1700, 95 percent of its population was agricultural, and most of this quite poor. Here were severe constraints on the development of consumerism. Even as these constraints moderated (and they still have not entirely disappeared, though urbanism and secularism are far more advanced), hesitations about consumerism persisted in various guises.

Russia's distinctiveness, then, was rooted in the tension between a social and economic structure badly prepared for consumerism, and a strong Western inclination. Consumerism developed early, reflecting the Western pull, but it developed incompletely and with great resistance. Debates still continue.

The background

It is hardly surprising that a highly peasant society generated far fewer indications of consumerism than, say, the great societies of Asia before the nineteenth century. Market trade and the use of money were not well developed, and exchanges largely focussed on necessities.

In 1701, as part of his selective westernization program, Peter the Great decreed that the Russian nobility must adopt Western dress. The decree led to a rapidly growing interest in acquiring fashionable clothing as a status symbol. The aristocracy led the way of course, but some merchants and non-aristocratic bureaucrats followed in their wake. By the nineteenth century, fashionable shops spread increasingly in the cities. Again, the bulk of the population was unaffected. Mostly unaware of the new elite interests, the masses of peasants resented the visible signs of aristocratic consumer wealth and foreign consumer focus.

There was, however, a new tension being established. Russian aristocrats, particularly the great magnates in the cities, were eager to match their

Western counterparts in living standards, which meant a growing interest not only in foreign tastes but in sheer acquisition. Clothing led the way, but furnishings and art objects were not far behind. Furthermore, most of the new shops were sponsored by foreign, and particularly French, capitalists. They coexisted with traditional Russian open markets used mainly by the lower classes. The French word for shops, *magazins*, reflected the segregation in buying patterns.

Traditional urban shopping, in the open markets, obviously involved consumption of a sort, but it was mainly focussed on necessities. It provided pleasure, but less through the goods than through the social process of dealing with shopkeepers, haggling, and seeing neighbors. As in other parts of the world, this kind of market activity differed from consumerism, and consumerism would ultimately compete with it. The tension between traditional urban markets and modern consumer forms – again, dramatic in Russia but visible in most other societies such as the Middle East – was an intriguing one. While the modern forms gained ground, older forms long coexisted. Even today, tourist interest in remaining open-air markets, and attempts to revive more personal kinds of sales settings, suggest some of the issues involved.

For traditional shopping was informal, with frequent heated exchanges between customers and clerks. It was unpredictable, spontaneous, and disorderly. Western-style shopping was cold and formal by contrast. Its pleasures lay in the goods themselves, and in keeping up with fashion in a new urban lifestyle developing through the nineteenth century. Shopping no longer involved necessities or social contacts with shopkeepers, so much as acquisition, seeing and being seen in a luxury setting, and the symbolic "dream worlds" that accumulated goods might inspire.

Russian department stores and their critics

It was the rapid changes in upper-class taste, and the extensive contact with Western merchants, that set the context for the surprisingly early arrival of department stores in the major cities by the 1850s. The stores built on elite consumerism, and they directly challenged the previous conventions of the urban markets. The first store was launched by a French merchant, and foreigners long dominated the major stores in Moscow's fashionable districts. Instead of shopkeepers shouting the glories of their wares, the new stores featured polite, well-dressed clerks and standardized prices; the whole bargaining process was abolished. Increasingly, the older types of stores seemed both unmodern and non-Western, a product of Russia's contacts with Asia.

The result led to more than the usual kinds of laments about modern consumerism, for the new stores seemed foreign to many Russians. One observer, writing around 1900, contrasted traditional market stalls and the modern *magazin*:

In this difference are the echoes of two changing systems of morals and manners. With the colossal houses, with the trams and automobiles, in general with the ascendancy of the machine, the former good nature, the conviviality, the appealing disorderliness and freedom are disappearing. The tenor of life is becoming disciplined, is being chained to the machine.

Other commentators bemoaned the spread of Western clothing fashions, again citing the impersonality involved. Russian clothes had been comfortable, but now people looked like factory products, for no reason except that everyone else was wearing the same styles. Again, as in reactions to consumerism elsewhere, a social status angle emerged: customary barriers were being brought down as stores and styles became open to various ranks.

Gender came in for comment, as in other cases. Many Russian authors commented on female frivolity, compared to the productive activities of men. Journalist Iulii Elets blamed female fixation on fashion as responsible for an overall moral decline in Russia, leading to the neglect of children and the victimization of hardworking husbands. He called women's obsession with consumerism an "epidemic insanity," spreading to all social classes. Major authors, such as Tolstoy, joined the parade of critics; a Tolstoy story linked women's new clothing with male sexual obsession and deep personal tragedy. "Women, like queens, have forced nine-tenths of the human race to labor for them as their slaves." Tolstoy and other authors saw high-fashion women as debauched, dressing like prostitutes and scarcely different from them in morals.

Obviously, the level of Russian criticism reflected but also obscured some real change. Most Russians still, around 1900, were far from the consumerist world, which was largely urban and disproportionately upper class. Women were hardly uniformly ensnared. But the criticisms did reflect growing interest in consumerism, and a linkage between consumer visibility and other trappings of modernity and civilization. The temptations of Western standards, as measurements of superiority, blended with other consumer enjoyments. Department stores helped a new urban population, including women, form an identity. A late-nineteenth-century observer commented on how Russian shop windows were "full of the inventions of Western civilization – easy chairs, statuettes, china, cravats, silk stockings, parasols, photographs of French actresses and ballet girls, yellow-covered French novels." Through consumerism, Western interests became available to wider segments of the population.

Even the countryside began to be drawn in. A 1904 article described a migrant peasant wearing Western style clothing, and his colleagues "looked on him as a marvel." But the criticisms loomed large as well, dominating commentary far more than in the contemporary West. Complaints of "dandyism" followed even the mildest sign of rural consumerism, as intellectuals held to a nostalgic valuation of peasant simplicity and virtue. A new generation of urban writers emerged in the early twentieth century, but they too expressed anxiety and uncertainty about consumer culture. The foreignness of the leading styles obviously focussed attention, as part of the standing Russian debate about whether West should be model or pariah, whether Russia must change or hew to superior values of its own.

The rise of a Russian leftwing, though partly inspired by Western ideas such as Marxism, added to the debate over consumerism. Karl Marx himself, writing near the middle of the nineteenth century in Germany and England, had not paid direct attention to consumerism. He focussed on the issues of the working class at the time, which involved survival, not handling the fruits of affluence. And his own life was lived in considerable poverty. There is no question that Marx and Marxism concentrated more directly on work and working conditions than on consumerism. Criticism of the exploitative middle class could include implications that consumerism was "bourgeois" and backward. But Marx and his followers could also imagine, if somewhat vaguely, improved access to consumerism as part of the legitimate rewards of labor in a revolutionary society. Marx's goals included the phrase, "from each according to his abilities, to each according to his needs," which conveyed his focus on improving access to the material necessities of life. This approach was not necessarily anti-consumerist. Marxism was quite different from fascism in this regard. Marx did hope that an industrial economy, operating in a communist rather than a capitalist system, would produce a better material life for the majority.

Russian communists, sincere Marxists but also operating in the Russian cultural context, were clearer: consumerism was a foreign imposition which merely increased the exploitation of the masses for the benefit of an elite. The huge and visible gaps between the well-to-do patrons of department stores and the masses of urban and rural poor made it easy to focus attacks on consumerism for contributing to gross inequality. Ironically, Marxists in this sense joined hands with nationalist conservatives, in attacking consumerism as a common enemy.

Consumerism in Soviet society

Against the checkered initial history of Russian consumerism, the triumph of the communists in the Revolution of 1917 ushered in a new set of constraints. Advancing consumerism was not a goal of the revolutionaries. In a society reeling from World War I and then the chaos of the revolution itself, it was hard to put the economy back together, much less to promote consumer advance. Communist leaders sought to restrict consumption in the interest of investment in further industrialization. But values were involved as well. As a matter of ideological stance, communist leaders continued to attack Western consumerism as a sign of the decadence and inequality of capitalist society. Consumerism from this standpoint was a frivolity for the wealthy few, while poverty and exploitation defined the lives of the majority even in the West. Communists urged collective rather than individual goals within the Soviet Union itself, which constrained consumerism from yet another angle. This is one of the reasons that Soviet industry, as it advanced, did not focus on consumer goods.

Under communism, particularly after Stalin assumed power, the resources of the Russian state were devoted to advancing industrialization, particularly in heavy industry. By the mid-1930s, additional funding had to go to the military, to respond first to the Nazi threat, then to World War II itself, and then to the operation of the Soviet empire and the challenge of the Cold War. Consumer goods production was systematically neglected in this process. For decades, products as basic as bathtub plugs were in short supply, because of the funds devoted to the economic infrastructure and military needs. Daily life for many Russians involved a struggle simply to find adequate goods to buy for life's necessities. Long lines at food shops became part of the routine. Overall, material standards did improve at several points under communism, in a society that had long been very poor, but systematic consumer advance was not part of the process.

Yet consumerism did not die away in Soviet society. A real ambivalence persisted. There were several reasons for this. In the first place, as industrialization did gain ground, there were some resources available above basic necessity and, furthermore, workers themselves needed rewards for their participation in the process. The Soviet state frequently promised improvements in living conditions, and it delivered in certain respects. For example, vacation opportunities increased, with state-run resorts on the Black Sea and other spots. The trips were seen as part of a collective reward, but they obviously relieved the heavy production emphasis of the Soviet version of communism.

Furthermore, communist party leaders themselves sought special consumer pleasures, as something of a new class structure emerged in a post-revolutionary context. A new bureaucratic elite began to emerge by the mid-1930s, and it sought some fruits of prosperity. Many officials acquired country vacation homes. In 1934 a luxury food store opened in Moscow, which began a trend of pricey and exclusive stores for party bigwigs, with luxury products including imports from abroad.

Finally, the image of Western standards refused to vanish. Again in the 1930s, the state sanctioned the idea of a prosperous life, defined in terms of the acquisition of goods, and used Western slogans and representations to advertise many consumer products. Films in the 1930s and 1940s glamorized consumption, and many Soviet citizens, particularly in Moscow, bought foreign-made items. Even in the countryside, where standards remained far more modest, New Year's eve brought increased gift giving, designed to reflect the nation's prosperity that highlighted commercial products including more fashionable clothing.

The result, obviously, was a set of anomalies. Consumer opportunities existed for Soviet leadership, but they were not openly acknowledged in a presumably classless society. Western society was routinely attacked for softness and decadence, but Western goods, sales methods, and standards continued to loom large. Huge gaps existed, even aside from the party leadership, between countryside and city, but large numbers of people were encouraged to see consumer gains, particularly in clothing styles, as rewards for good work.

The best way to interpret consumerism in Soviet society involves assessing an effort to construct an alternative to Western consumerism. This process generated some parallels with the West, but also important differences, which were further exacerbated by the obvious fact that, throughout the Soviet era, consumerism took a lower priority to rapid industrialization and, during the Cold War, expansion of military expenditure.

The first moves, following the 1917 revolution, were pretty obvious. The state seized the old department stores. Not only private ownership but focus on an elite clientele could not persist in the revolutionary environment. Various state enterprises were installed instead, and they initially trumpeted a new, communist approach to consumerism in which outlets would be available to everyone. The new shoppers were to come from "the working population" of city and countryside alike. Advertisements featured peasants looking at stylish overcoats. State-sponsored stores were typically large – the communists wanted size and efficiency in the most up-to-date manner, and the department store model worked well here. The goal was to supply all the needs of the citizens. One store thus touted, "Clothe the body, feed the stomach, fill the mind, Everything a person needs."

Amid the new appeals to ordinary people, Soviet consumerism developed some features similar to those in the West. Increasing numbers of women were recruited as sales clerks. They were assumed to be cleaner than men, more in tune with customer wishes particularly on the domestic side of things. Another similarity showed up in some advertisements. A 1923 ad, for example, claimed, "A Person is a Person only with a Watch. The only Watch to Own is a Mozer." Modern quality of life and consumer goals were identical here, as in consumerism in other parts of the world.

But there were distinctions as well, beginning of course with the limitations on consumer goods production and availability. The new stores also emphasized worker rights as opposed to customer service, arguing that the old bourgeois system, in which clerks were supposed to defer to customers, was unfair to labor. Many Soviet stores, despite their claims, turned out to feature limited and often poor quality products backed by surly, inattentive sales personnel. Complaints about inadequacy multiplied – it was at least possible to complain, though state bureaucrats normally rejected the pleas, claiming they were "unfounded" or "groundless." ("Does not correspond to reality" was a favorite dismissing phrase.)

Consumer appetites, but also characteristic limitations, showed up in what became the greatest Russian department store. A major Moscow store, initially called the Upper Trading Rows, had opened in 1907. Under the communists the store was renamed GUM (*gosudarstvennyj universal'nyi magazin*, or state department store). During the 1920s GUM operated more like a large bazaar, in the traditional Russian mode, but then it became increasingly more similar to Western department stores. Shopping in GUM was presented as a pleasurable activity, with considerable focus on atmosphere. Like the department stores in Asia discussed in the next chapter, and more than in the West, GUM housed cultural performances throughout the Soviet era as part of its overall operation. GUM also participated eagerly in the new Soviet holidays.

The store became one of the largest in the world. By the 1950s it boasted over 130,000 customers a day, second only to Macy's in New York. But the goods for sale did not live up to the building or the ambiance, either in quality or availability. Clerks continued to tote up sales on the abacus because there were no cash registers. Clothing was the most expensive category available. Food, books, and appliances were cheap. A television set cost the same as two cheap suits, but in fact few were actually available and the quality was poor. Communist Party stalwarts more commonly shopped at outlets available only to them, where more imported goods were supplied. GUM became something of an attraction for Western tourists as the Cold War eased, but they went less for consumer joys than as an exploration of the deficiencies of the Russian consumer economy.

Department stores and consumer production were not, of course, the whole story. In building an alternative society, Soviet leaders intended to provide satisfactions other than Western-style consumerism. It was cheap and easy, for example, to travel throughout the huge country, and many people were able to take vacations to Moscow or St Petersburg. The organized excursions to the Black Sea gave workers an alternative to normal daily routines. Welfare protections were designed to assist in illness or old age. Wide distribution of medals, for state service of various sorts including productive work, provided an alternative set of rewards, and they were often proudly displayed. Greater use of uniforms, not only for the military but for communist youth and other groups, provided alternatives to changes and individualism in clothing styles. Consumerism in anything like the Western style had a different, clearly lesser, role to play in this overall social package.

Ongoing ambivalence: 1950s–2000

After the Stalinist era passed, and even more as Cold War tensions lessened, openings for consumer interest increased. There were two main developments. In the first place, communist leaders tended to move away from attacks on Western decadence, toward a sense that Soviet society itself should be producing higher consumer standards as part of communist success. A fascinating glimpse of change occurred during the visit to the United States of the post-Stalinist premier, Nikita Krushchev, in 1959 – the first such visit of a Soviet leader. Krushchev was shown a variety of wonders of American consumerism. His reaction – and it was a plausible one at the time, given the fact that Russian economic growth rates were higher than those in the United States – suggested that the Soviet Union would soon surpass American levels. "We will bury you" was his somewhat menacing, but largely competitive cry; he seemed to mean a Soviet future in which automobiles and other American staples would become abundant. Not all facets of American consumerism pleased the visitor – a Hollywood set filled with scantily clad dancers drew moralistic disapproval about decadence – but Khrushchev's overall reaction suggested a commitment to communist-style consumerism. Later Russian leaders maintained similar hints, including one with a personal passion for collecting fast cars.

The second new component involved more ordinary Soviet citizens, in a context in which knowledge of Western standards began to grow. The result was selective, but increasingly influential. Groups of Western tourists began to visit Soviet cities, providing knowledge about Western clothing styles. Access to films, rock music, and other artifacts increased somewhat. Among many youths, Western consumer culture seemed to provide an alternate identity, and efforts to buy products like blue jeans symbolized changing expectations. Specific Western icons could now be set up: a McDonald's opened in Moscow, attracting huge throngs despite relatively high prices. Revealingly, one of the innovations McDonald's brought, besides the food, involved explicit training in cheerful customer service.

The Fall of Communism

Consumer challenges did not bring down the communist system. Far more important were environmental degradation and the huge burden of military expenditures as the Cold War progressed. Almost half of the national product was going to the military by the 1980s, at obvious cost to other sectors, and this was not sustainable. But consumer inadequacies played a role in undermining the system. It proved increasingly difficult to motivate workers, and lack of consumer rewards and (particularly for women) the sheer burden of daily shopping helped explain this fact. Alcoholism increased, which simply added to the dysfunction of the economy. The Soviet effort to create an alternative to a Western-style consumer society did not ultimately succeed.

Then came the changes in economic and political policy under Mikhail Gorbachev, from 1985 onward, that ultimately led to the collapse of the Soviet system. And the result of change, in increasing and regularizing knowledge of Western standards, opened consumer interests still further. Large numbers of Russian business people – often called "new Russians" – began to use growing money earnings to indulge in the joys of Western-style consumer life, complete with an array of imported amenities and products. Stores changed, with a far greater range of products and cheerful, colorful displays. Urban women began to dress more elegantly – often outdoing their American counterparts, where comfort and informality had gained a greater hold. The goal of moving toward a modern consumer society, never fully repressed, now seemed dominant.

But still there were hesitations. For many Russians, including large numbers of workers, soldiers, and the elderly, continued or even growing privation prevented any real participation in consumerism, in an economy that was poor and seriously ailing. There were signs as well that some Russians did not want consumerism even if it were available. An increase in religious interest drew a few. Even more reported resentments at the consumer success of some of their colleagues, arguing that equality was more important than individual expression. Neither the economic nor the cultural foundations for consumerism were yet fully established. The old debate was recast, the critical voices more scattered; but it had not ended.

In the process of a long and hesitant flirtation with consumerism, thanks to a complex pre-modern experience and the vivid Soviet interlude, Russia had turned out to lag in consumer development, not only behind the West but behind many nations in Asia and Latin America. The Russian case, clearly, involved unusual historical complexity, and the uncertain prospects for the twenty-first century highlighted complexity as well.

Further reading

S. Boym, *Common Places: Mythologies of Everyday Life in Russia* (Cambridge, MA: Harvard University Press, 1994); D.R. Brower, *The Russian City Between Tradition and Modernity, 1850–1900* (Berkeley, CA: University of California Press, 1990); Sheila Fitzpatrick, *The Cultural Front: Power and Culture in Revolutionary Russia* (Ithaca, NY: Cornell University Press, 1992); John Gunther, *Inside Russia Today* (London: H. Hamilton, 1998); Kelly and David Shephard, eds, *Constructing Russian Culture in the Age of Revolution: 1881–1940* (New York: Oxford University Press, 1998); Christine Ruane, "Clothes shopping in Imperial Russia: the development of a consumer culture," *Journal of Social History* 28: 765–782 (Pittsburgh, PA: Carnegie Mellon University Press, 1995); R. Stites, *Russian Popular Culture: Entertainment and Society Since 1990* (New York: Cambridge University Press, 1992). On the GUM stores, Marjorie Hilton, "Retailing the Revolution: The State Department Store (GUM) and Soviet Society in the 1920s," *Journal of Social History* 37: 939–964.

Chapter 8

Consumerism in East Asia

This chapter deals with the rise of modern consumerism in China and Japan, where some elements of consumerism had already been suggested, even affecting the West at an earlier point in time. Chinese and Japanese experiences differed, despite a common context that particularly involved significant Confucian influence. Both patterns contrasted with Russia, though there was a shared concern about the foreign and disruptive qualities of consumer interests.

There are internal contrasts as well. Comparisons of China and Japan in the nineteenth and twentieth centuries are common, and they are revealing. It is no secret that China resisted significant change even as Western interference grew. Japan, in contrast, reacted swiftly, altering political and economic forms by the 1870s. Consumerism mirrors some of these broader differences. China held back from consumerism for several reasons. Japan hardly rushed to consumerism as rapidly as it embraced, say, changes in education, military structures, or public health, but many Japanese saw elements of consumerism as a natural part of their broader admiration for Western values and as rewards for the arduous experience of change in other spheres. Despite this, Japan was no carbon copy of Western consumerism. Different from China, for reasons that must be carefully explored, Japan also adopted the Western version of consumerism selectively.

Both China and Japan were largely agricultural societies when Western influence accelerated, though cities and urban classes were important. Both contained considerable poverty, and for some people poverty increased due to Western exploitation (in China) or the costs of economic development (in Japan). Here were important constraints on a rapid conversion to consumerism, holding even Japan back from a full capacity to match the West in consumer range. Cultural elements also limited and guided consumerism in these two societies. Elements of Confucian tradition clearly explain some of the delays in full adoption of consumerism, as well as some of the anxieties consumer behaviors could create; but cultural factors also guided the ways consumerism managed to develop. Economic factors were also vital: Japan industrialized on the basis of extensive exports, essential to pay for vital imports of raw materials and fuel; this created a context in which the government long discouraged too much internal consumerism or consumer production lest it distract from the export thrust. A similar pattern emerged in China after 1978. These economic policies would not necessarily discourage elaborate consumerism forever: Japan, certainly, broke through the context by the twenty-first century, though still with some hesitations including a consistently high rate of personal savings. The East Asian contexts for consumerism resulted from several key components.

China: resistance and later impacts

Prior to the eighteenth century, European consumer items had scant impact on Asia. A great deal of trade followed traditional patterns, independent of European intermediaries, and the range of goods Europe had to offer was limited. Silver, brought from the New World, and a certain amount of weaponry counted for more than new consumer products. By the late eighteenth century, however, the extension of European power drew some interest toward wider fashions. Portraits of certain upper-class Indian ladies, for example, show them in European style dress, stiffly posed as if constrained by the unfamiliarity. This degree of consumer interest and opportunity remained unusual, but it signaled some new influences.

Well into the nineteenth century, however, the impact of European consumer interests on China specifically continued to be a one-way street. European traders sought a wide range of Chinese goods, from porcelain to tea, for the growing markets back home, but they had little they could induce the Chinese to buy in exchange. In addition to continued imports of Mexican silver, some of which was fashioned into jewelry for elite buyers, the key European import into the later nineteenth century turned out to be opium. The spread of opium use had, to be sure, some consumer-like features. Many initial buyers came from the wealthy upper classes, particularly among young men, and they were seeking novelty and diversion. In the long run, however, quite apart from bitter if not always effective official opposition to opium use, opium did not encourage wider consumer patterns. Its mind-numbing qualities discouraged consumer desire rather than fanning it further. An eighteenth-century edict against opium use explicitly noted how purchasers "continually become sunk into the most stupid and besotted state," and this was hardly the context for wider consumer behavior. Opium imports flourished, with Chinese merchants collaborating with European and American smugglers. This became, by the 1830s, the world's largest trade in any single commodity. With Western governments insisting on their right to promote the trade, China's increasingly ineffective government was powerless to resist strongly. Only at the end of the nineteenth century did increasing domestic production cut imports, though not necessarily usage.

China did resist or ignore more general inducements toward new forms of consumerism - precisely the reason that Westerners decided that they had to focus so fiercely on drugs. The kinds of goods that attracted Russians or various Native American groups simply had little appeal. There were three reasons for the marked and durable gap between European consumer habits and Chinese reactions. The first involved massive poverty in a largely rural society in which population was growing rapidly: China simply lacked the economic basis for the kind of consumerism developing in Europe, particularly in the countryside. But the other two factors counted as well, given the large size of Chinese cities and the importance of a wealthy upper class. The first factor was economic, the second cultural; and they operated in some mutual tension.

China already had, not a consumer society in the Western sense, but well developed consumer products. An English merchant noted that China already seemed to have everything: "the best food in the world, rice; the best drink, tea; and the best clothing, cotton, silk, fur." Many European products, such as "china," were just pale imitations of what China already produced. Even cotton goods (which ultimately provided some inroad) were better made in China than in the growing European factories, into the 1830s. China needed a few consumer raw materials from other places, such as lead for tea chests; pepper; and cane for beds and chairs, but these could be obtained through established trading patterns in South East Asia and hardly encouraged either an interest in Western items or some new surge of consumerism.

It was true that the eighteenth century saw the spread of upper-class life styles to a growing number of wealthy families in the cities. Garden villas became more popular – extensive gardens with pavilions, bridges, ponds, and winding walkways. This was consumerism of a sort, in terms of suggesting interests in more opulent lifestyles, but the fashions involved were highly traditional. The same trends applied to food and clothing, where materialism might spread but not the zest for novelty and frantic acquisition typical of consumerism in the contemporary West. Clothing fashions did change periodically, based on the tastes of trend-setting elites in the big cities; and there were other innovations, such as growing use of restaurants. But court dress remained stable, defined by customary stand-ards, and many furnishing styles, like architecture itself, demonstrated a long and conservative tradition. And of course the groups involved were far smaller as a percentage of total population than the expanding consumer audience in Western Europe.

These constraints related to the second, cultural factor. China continued to display a vigorous if oscillating concern about regulating displays of materialism in the interest both of appropriate, traditional social hierarchy and of the higher public values of Confucianism. Attacks on "decadence" and "extravagance" accompanied every hint of greater acquisitiveness, as in the eighteenth century. Thus an official in 1781 blasted wasteful expenditures in taverns and teahouses. In this case the Emperor disagreed, claiming that "customs daily become more extravagant but the situation cannot be altered by law," but in a culture dependent on citations from the past, older attacks on display could constantly be revived. Thus a Confucian legacy argued that "wise kings and imperial rulers did not treasure rarities or value goods which were difficult to obtain" (two potential bases for consumerism), urging instead that economic focus remain on items that were useful and necessary to life. Others cited the example of an earlier (Ming dynasty) emperor who worried that greed and covetousness would lead to social decay and even the extinction of family lines, and who destroyed some fancy carriages as a result. There were past statutes as well, regulating in great detail what kinds of goods each rank in the elite could legitimately own – gold goblets instead of jade for one set of high officials for example, no silver utensils at all for merchants or artisans. Gaudy clothing, in particular, was frequently taken as a sign of decadence, in a cultural tradition going back to the classical period.

Widespread poverty and existing consumer satisfactions combined with cultural concern about undue display or the mixing of social lines created the context in which a further escalation into Western-style consumerism did not occur, despite growing Western pressure and presence into the later nineteenth century. This does not mean that there was no change, quite apart from the spread of opium. Wealthy groups in the city did pick up new tastes in clothing, including brighter and more varied colors, and in artistic furnishings during the eighteenth century, and there was no attempt literally to revive the older legal controls. The use of wine with meals spread, even for many common people in the cities. So did tobacco smoking, usually in a water pipe but sometimes, for upper-class people aware of European elite fashions, as snuff. None of this created a market for European products, but it did further blur the distinction between urban buying habits and a tentative Chinese version of a consumer society.

The first serious inroads of European manufactured imports, however, did not really push consumerism further, for they involved replacement of the source for an existing item: cotton cloth, rather than a new splurge of consumer behavior. Imported, factory-made cotton cloth increasingly cut into Chinese domestic production that had become well-established as early as the sixteenth century. Many people were thrown out of work in this process. There were, however, two further results that hinted at more openness to other forms of consumerism. First, while fashions in cotton clothing remained regional, there was the possibility, given European production origins, of new colors or other modifications. Second, Chinese merchants in cities like Shanghai, that had long depended on domestic cotton trade, were obviously in the market for new activities.

Further Western commercial pressure in the later nineteenth century, including the outright acquisition of a number of port regions such as

Hong Kong increased the impetus for change. By the 1870s some shops in cities like Shanghai specialized in "Western merchandise." When they started in the 1840s, they carried only a few machine-made cottons, but by the 1870s their range expanded to include a much wider array. Other new imports came from Japan, including knives and tobacco items. Some merchants, and also extortionist gangs called *tang*, resisted these trends, insisting on the primacy of more traditional and Chinese-made goods. Soon after 1900 the great Boxer rebellion, sponsored in part by government officials, attacked many forms of Western influence, among them imported cotton cloth. "Foreign goods" were one of the Boxers' explicit targets, along with "foreign matters" such as railways, telegraphs, and imported weapons.

Clearly, some highly commercial Chinese centers, under Western influence, were moving toward greater consumerism but the trend was resisted and constrained by widespread poverty (some of which the Western imports exacerbated) and anti-foreign resistance.

The diverse trends of the twentieth century

The first Western-style department stores were established in Chinese commercial cities under Western control and through the efforts of Chinese businessmen with experience in places such as Hawaii and, particularly, Australia. Hong Kong led the way, under British control, featuring an array of imported Western goods. Overseas Chinese merchants from Australia took the lead soon after in Guangzhou and Shanghai. More traditional shops selling well-known products concentrated in particular parts of town (tobacco stores and paper-product stores were particularly viable), persisted as well, but department stores offered not only a greater range of goods but also lower, fixed prices. Department stores helped instruct consumers, particularly women, from various social classes in the essentials of a modern lifestyle, including Chinese plus European fashions as well as foodstuffs from literally around the world. By the 1920s department stores such as Sincere and Sun Sun, in Shanghai, were architectural monuments, but also centers of cosmopolitan culture including the city's first ballroom and its first radio station. Consumer goods were linked to new, commercial leisure styles. An effort to use women as sales clerks, however, drew too much unfavorable attention and was dropped for a time. Further, the stores also encouraged Chinese crafts, such as lacquer work and ivory carving, offering prizes for good workmanship. Here was something of a compromise in a Western dominated consumer style.

By the 1920s Shanghai was leading the nation in fashion-setting, with suits based on the styles of political leaders rivaling outright Western imports. Skirt lengths changed annually, the same emblem of fickle consumerism and its female focus that could be found in the contemporary West. French-style coffeehouses spread widely (imitating the eighteenth-century European trend), with strong patronage from intellectuals and publishers interested in pursuing Western trends in writing and commercial distribution. Advertisements featured American-type family promotion, implying that use of Colgate toothpaste and laundry soap, plus Quaker Oats, would maintain family unity and keep the children healthy. American movies spread as well, usually winning mediocre reviews, they nevertheless typically commanded eight or nine of the top ten sales slots. A nationalist writer had to admit that, partly because of lack of funding, "Chinese movies are really not as good as foreign movies" even as the latter commanded growing audiences. At the same time, Shanghai suffered from a widespread belief that it was becoming "unChinese," that its commercialism somehow tainted it. Even within Shanghai, most people continued to shop in neighborhood outlets, rarely if ever venturing to the big downtown stores. When asked why, a group of lifelong Shanghai residents noted that they lacked the time for window-shopping and "We have nothing to buy there." It was revealing that the key new stores, on Nanking Road, bordered the residential area for foreigners. A profound ambivalence about consumerism persisted among the Chinese themselves. A few products, such as commercial calendars, which imitated Western forms but used Chinese artistic themes, tried to bridge the gap explicitly.

The expansion of consumerism and the consumer apparatus was furthered by the leader of the Chinese revolution of 1911, Sun Yat-sen, himself an investor in a department store. Not a mindless Westernizer, Sun nevertheless promoted wider distribution of goods as a key component of his modernization program. The spread of department stores featuring many products would be fundamental to greater prosperity. But there were countercurrents. Nationalist pressures led to widespread boycotts of British goods in the 1920s, which cut into department store sales. In general, in China but also India and elsewhere, consumer boycotts worked much better than they did in the West, because consumerism was less deeply rooted and because it presented a foreign target. More important was the advent of the Communist regime in 1949, officially dedicated to values of production and the creation of a more egalitarian society, not to consumerism. The state took over department stores, and even founded a new one, the Emporium, in the capital city, Beijing. Some of these turned into showcases for Chinese-made products of various sorts, though the possibilities of consumerism more generally suffered and the stores could sustain themselves only by government assistance in procuring scarce items. During the Cultural Revolution, 1966–1975, the armed Red Guards banned a number of traditional products, such as religious decorations, and also consumer items with Western names or connections (such as woolen clothing or whiskey). High-heeled shoes, mechanical toys, and playing cards were also banned (cards a symbol of distraction, despite the fact that the Chinese had long ago invented them).

Overall, the communist movement, particularly under Mao Zedong, constituted a great reversal for consumerism in China. Officially, the reasons were largely new, though continued poverty still played a role. Implicitly, as in other respects, the movement built on some older traditions in Chinese culture that in this case urged against undue devotion to materialism or personal spending.

From their revolutionary days in rural provinces to their full takeover, communist leaders emphasized production rather than consumption. The goal was not an economic foundation which would later yield consumer fruits, but production for the social good; and the sense of social contribution was to be its own reward. Even the army was enjoined to "engage in production" in intervals between fighting. Two related goals involved opposition to luxury and any upper-class indulgence, a natural outgrowth of a sincere communist ideology, and a desire to eliminate dependence on foreign imports. Imports had, in the words of one communist writer, rendered China a "semi colonial state" for a long time, and the political costs were not worth the access to frivolous items. Production of consumer goods, beyond the needs of normal living, was typically destined for export, to earn foreign exchange – a new version of an older Chinese pattern.

In fact, attacks not only on imports but also on private business more generally, plus frequent production bottlenecks, severely hampered the national economy and naturally restricted domestic consumerism – even aside from official policy. Many stores, including the principal state-run operations, had to make special under the table deals to acquire any goods at all. Shortages were so great that when items such as television sets were due to appear, the meager supplies were exhausted in advance. Personal connections, called *guanxi*, were a precondition of even modest consumer success. The few products available were often exceptionally shoddy – handles came off cups, dishes disintegrated – the result of limitations on manufacturing capacity but also the official lack of interest in the consumer sector. Clothing displayed little variety – a white shirt or a Mao jacket with blue or gray trousers for men; wristwatches were the only sign of personal ornamentation for either gender. The result was a homogeneity that fitted in with emphasis on collective rather than individual identity. Housing, finally, was state-run, with private construction eliminated; the result, again, was a gray uniformity, though also a reduction of some of the worst urban slums. The communist system did not lower standards for everyone, but it did work against consumerism at every level. Scarcity and communist ideology combined.

This was not the final chapter in what turns out to be an oscillating set of national reactions to the threat or potential of modern consumerism. Changes in policy toward expanding the role of a market economy began to be introduced in 1978, and an explosion of consumer interest followed. Economic levels now permitted greater consumerism, particularly by young urban professionals but to some extent more widely. Communist attempts to dampen consumer interests clearly had not eliminated the impulse – it was fascinating that earlier centers, such as Shanghai, quickly reemerged as style-setters. Consumerism was also essential to motivate people amid rapid, disorienting change. Special factors also operated: strict limitations on birthrates made parents eager to indulge the few children they had, a key context for consumerism and for its steady enhancement with each new generation. By the mid-1980s, when consumer imports became possible, an early target for the rising urban middle classes involved children's toys and clothing from the West, held to be distinctively fashionable. Finally, China's opening led to new levels of foreign commercial operation, making American consumerism, particularly, something of a standard in many areas (though with some interesting local twists). In comparison with the long Maoist era, and to some extent even to pre-communist Chinese history, observers at home and abroad could note a real consumer revolution.

Symptoms were wide ranging. For business and professional people making significant incomes under the new system, housing became more elaborate, which in turn created appetites for new types of decoration and appliances. New advertisements, admittedly at the luxury end of the scale, evoked French charm:

> Every time when you get a taste from television or books of the magnificent Louvre Palace, the relaxing murmur of the Seine River you always hope that one day you can own a home like that, with all the romantic style of France.

Wutong Gardens, opening in 1997, would give buyers just that feel, in "typical French architectural style" with furnished rooms decorated in the fashion of the Middle Ages. Department stores, virtually empty of goods just a few years before, now had whole sections devoted to electronic games. Stores such as the Emporium regained the opportunity to feature a wide variety of products and services, including luxury items. Following foreign examples, various "shops in the store" were created, for supermarket activities, sale of high fashion, electric appliances and the like. Personal appearance won new attention, with elaborate cosmetics and beauty salons (the salons employed five million people by 1998) as well as varied, often Western-style clothing. Sex shops sold their own range of goods. Commercial greeting cards became popular. Many were wrapped in cellophane, so that when opened they would emit a perfumed scent. Young women called friends to tell them they had sent a card, indicating the price in hopes their friends would send back something even more expensive. The goal was conspicuous consumption and display of affluence.

Ownership of bicycles and television sets proliferated. In major cities, over a third of all young adults had pagers. As in all consumer societies, gradations of wealth were mirrored in what one could buy: the affluent were moving on to motorcycles, automobiles, and air conditioners. Children rivaled each other in displays of toys.

Advertisements proliferated for virtually every imaginable product, including a spectacular series for American Marlboro cigarettes using a traditional Chinese martial arts dance as a backdrop. Soft contact lenses transform a middle school student into a lovely girl. Apollo, a sun tonic, will give new energy (for men only – in Chinese custom, the power of the sun is a male symbol). Revealingly, none of the ads spoke in terms of patriotism or revolutionary spirit; all emphasized comfort and personal identity.

Restaurant eating became more common. American fast-food outlets were a new rage, with a few Chinese wannabes, such as Red Sorghum, lagging a bit behind. Interestingly, the patrons did not particularly like the food involved. One loyal patron noted, "The Big Mac doesn't taste great; but the experience of eating in this place makes me feel good. Sometimes I even imagine that I am sitting in a restaurant in New York or Paris." Here was a key way for successful young professionals to define themselves, creating a display and a fantasy at the same time. The fast-food outlets suggested modernity and equality as well as unusually friendly service and hygiene. Many people, belying the fast food part, sat in the restaurants for hours, soaking up the atmosphere, seeing and being seen.

There were constraints, of course. Consumerism was mainly urban, in a nation still predominantly rural and impoverished. Villages changed as well, with more telephones and other innovations, but real consumerism was reserved for a minority of market-oriented farmers. Even a successful chicken farmer spent sparingly, buying a radio cassette recorder so his daughter could study for college examinations, but otherwise avoiding electric appliances in favor of putting his money into expanded production. Not only production, but also village and Communist Party progress meant more to this rural capitalist than consumerism. Even in the cities consumerism was new in a society still dominated by a communist political system and with a tradition of oscillation and recurrent resentment of foreignness. The government itself held back consumerism in the cities. Despite growing prosperity and huge export earnings, many officials were rewarded with collective trips abroad rather than the incomes that would permit wider and more individualistic consumer spending. Communist thinking here combined with older Confucian restraints, not to prevent consumerism but to limit it. Certainly, when constraints and poverty are added together, China's role in producing consumer goods for the world market grew far more rapidly than internal activity did.

Without question, a consumer revolution was occurring in China by the late twentieth century, in a surprisingly short span of time. Its success showed in the blend of Chinese themes and tastes with foreign markets. But only the future could define its extent and durability.

Japan

Like China, Japan offered some important elements of consumerism before the modern era and its Western contacts. There were also some limitations, including the considerable poverty of most ordinary people and the large gap between urban and rural cultures. But it is legitimate to inquire whether even pre-reform Japan leaned a bit further toward consumerism than China did, as part of the explanation of Japan's greater embrace from the late nineteenth century onward.

Pre-modern consumer forms

Urban Japan benefited from steady commercial growth during the seventeenth and eighteenth centuries, though the vast majority of the population continued to live in the countryside. Economic expansion supported the development of earlier urban cultural forms that in turn had consumer implications. The *kabuki* theater, for example, drew audiences from both elite and mass sectors within cities such as Edo. The plays themselves provided enjoyment, and they inspired other products. Woodcut prints of famous actors sold widely. They appealed among other things to many women, some of whom were clearly star-struck. Fashion worn by actors and actresses also provided models for more general fads. In the eighteenth century, one leading actor wore a new design with the symbol of a sickle and the syllables *wa* and *nu*, the whole spelling out the word *kamawanu*, or "I don't care." The symbol spread widely in the clothing shops, just as the production of a large variety of dyed fabrics and kimonos increased. *Kabuki* plays even harbored advertisements, for various brand-name rice crackers for example, used as the names of characters and then attributed to leading shops in the program notes. *Kabuki*, in sum, represented much of a consumer package, well before the impact of Western contact and the other modern impulses toward consumerism.

Japanese printing generated consumer items. Various books were widely sold, and new titles added to the appeal. Illustrated storybooks were common, and bookstores dominated some commercial neighborhoods in Edo and Kyoto. A given title might run into several thousand copies sold. Rising rates of literacy – Japan had the most literate population in the world outside the West by the eighteenth century, surging well ahead of China – helped sustain the book as a commercial object. Even more widespread was a popular artistic print known as *ukiyo-zoshi*. These were decorative sheets designed for pleasure, and produced cheaply enough for mass sales. There was no religious connotation, unlike earlier prints in Asia and Europe alike. *Ukiyo-zoshi* depicted urban and natural scenes, actors, aristocratic hunts, and samurai battles. Another consumer interest gaining ground in the eighteenth and early nineteenth centuries was the sushi stand, a common urban outlet during summer months.

Although Confucianism was advancing rapidly in this same period in Japan, becoming the leading cultural framework, the surges in outright consumerism were notable. Indeed, Confucian tracts often included some of the *ukiyo-zoshi* illustrations that book buyers or even renters could cut out for use as home decorations. Japanese commercial expansion, though not clearly more active than that in China, may have included fewer traditional constraints on consumer spending. Higher literacy was involved in key consumer interests and products, including some forms of advertising. Equally interesting was the growth of Western influence during the eighteenth century. Though Japan remained largely isolated, trade with Dutch merchants in the port of Nagasaki gave some Japanese wider contacts. Among the beneficiaries were several of the popular book publishers and illustrators. Thus one publisher, Suwaraya Ichibee, issued both stories and Western-inspired popularized science and medical tracts, plus fanciful travel tales under headings such as *Illustrations and Explanations of Myriad Nations* or *Miscellaneous Tales of Barbarians*. Here too was a trend absent from contemporary China.

Despite government efforts to control markets, lively popular sales had developed by 1800 in food products such as sugar and tea, but also textiles, pottery, and hardware. Consumerism was clearly escaping some of the controls of social hierarchy.

Japan was not a full-fledged consumer haven, even in the cities. Cultural and political constraints could still play a part, based on the preservation of firm social and gender hierarchy and on Confucian definitions of virtue. Thus as late as 1842 the government issued an edict limiting the subject matter of the *ukiyo-zoshi*. Prints of actors and geisha were forbidden as "detrimental to public morals." "In the future you are to select designs that are based on loyalty and filial piety and which serve to educate women and children. And you must ensure that they are not luxurious." The edict hit at the heart of the commercial print world, and it was followed by other restrictions on format and low prices. Here was more than a hint of the same kind of oscillation concerning consumer values that was present in China. More important still were direct attacks on popular spending, with an 1825 edict aimed at "presumptuous luxury" as the source of bad morals and corruption. Efforts continued to limit foreign contact, for the government feared that "mean and lowly" Japanese would be attracted to novel and exotic goods smuggled in by Western seamen.

Consumerism and modernization

New levels of Western contact washed over Japan from 1853 onward. While later in time than the Western pressures on China, and involving some of the same objectionable aspects of compulsion, the result brought a far quicker and more positive response to consumerism in the Japanese case, as part of the larger reform process. This was not a complete consumer triumph nor a purely Western version, but contact with the West did bring two vital components to Japan: a taste for new types of products and related openness to novelty, plus business experiences that provided a number of Japanese merchants with a detailed knowledge of Western consumer forms.

It is vital to note that consumerism did not drive Japan's commitment to change. Concern with national independence and the power of the state motivated selective Westernization, not a desire for material self-expression. Even with Westernization, great efforts were made to limit individualism in favor of nationalism and reverence for the Emperor. By the 1880s school curricula were filled with attacks on excessive selfishness or personal pre-occupation, a theme that has persisted into the present day. In addition to cultural constraints, massive and in some cases increasing poverty obviously limited consumerist potential for many decades. Japanese industrialization was successful, but it occurred on the backs of workers and peasants, including (and often particularly involving) women. High taxes and low wages made survival a challenge for many people until well after World War II.

Contacts with the West did open new interests, particularly of course in the cities. Many Japanese copied Western fashions as part of the effort to become modern. Western-style haircuts replaced the samurai shaved head with a topknot. Western standards of hygiene spread, and the Japanese became enthusiastic tooth-brushers and consumers of patent medicines. Clothing styles spread more slowly than haircuts, but Western influences arrived here too, and the first chair was installed in a public building in 1871.

Consumer involvements increased with time, partly because the outreach of Western consumer operations expanded – movies would play a significant role here. By the 1920s, not only Western styles of dress, but also sports and music fads gained acceptance in the cities. Baseball headed the list of new spectator sports (a Japanese schoolboy team beat a US navy group as early as the 1890s, to great national delight). Fashionable residents of Tokyo, eager to mimic the latest Western fashion, were called *maden boi* and *modan garu* (modern boy or girl). It is true that the "modern girls" idea was more a target for attacks against deterioration of traditional femininity than a reality, but the mixture reflected a transitional period in Japanese consumerism.

There were outright critics all along who argued that Japanese consumerism was destroying national values and national identity. As late as 1970 an intellectual critic, Yukio Mishima, who had devoted himself to traditional martial arts and founded a private army in defense of Japanese ideals, committed ritual suicide, claiming: "I came to wish to sacrifice myself for this old beautiful tradition of Japan, which is disappearing very quickly day by day."

Department stores

The rise of Japanese department stores, clearly in advance of their Chinese counterparts, tells the story of Japanese consumerism clearly: great interest, combined with ongoing efforts to preserve distinctive elements amid imitation of Western forms, and, more interestingly, considerable public hesitation that could only be overcome with special effort.

The Japanese department store first emerged in the decade after 1900 (it is important to note that this was more than thirty years after the commitment to reform), and it was seen by many as another sign of "civilization and enlightenment" as Japan moved closer to Western styles. Though clearly an import, and different from previous merchant customs, the department store personified the aspirations of the new middle class and intellectual community for self-fulfillment and gracious living. As in the West, the store brought new retailing methods by displaying goods and featuring a wide variety, by combining sales with other activities including exhibitions and advertising, by allowing shoppers to pick out goods directly, by pricing uniformly rather than encouraging bargaining, and by using large numbers of women sales clerks.

The first store formed when a clothing outlet took the name Misukoshi and proclaimed that it would be like "an American department store." The store's founder, Takahishi Sadao, had been trained in the United States, had studied Wanamaker's store in Philadelphia and was devoted to a Japanese consumer revolution. He and other imitators in what became Tokyo's modern shopping area brought in large numbers of families and women with children for day-long shopping excursions. Emphasis on fashion increased, copied from Paris. What was called a "dandy pattern" was introduced, using well-known geisha girls as models and promoting the notion that it was important to shift to new styles on an annual basis. These were, to be sure, Japanese fashions, the kimono, hair pins, and other goods, sprinkled with a few Western items such as ties for men. Advertising expanded, and by 1910 all the stores were publishing their own public relations magazines that stressed the importance of up-to-date fashion for daily life. Billboards and illuminated signs complemented the approach. An early campaign involved posters in train stations throughout the country around a "famous beauty" theme. By this point department stores were both benefiting from ongoing Japanese industrialization, with its outpouring of products and its profits for a growing middle class, and encouraging the same process by expanding the market for consumer goods. By 1908 stores such as Mitsukoshi were selling clothing, furnishings, art, and food; by 1922 the list had expanded to fifty departments, including Western-style furniture, cosmetics, toys, stationery, and musical instruments; by 1929, ninety-eight departments had added electrical appliances, furs, watches, bicycles, arts and crafts, and baby goods. Stores of this sort were housed in huge, eye-catching buildings, frequently reconstructed (highly modern features and elegant restrooms were key features, along with the nation's first escalator), and they were generating their own brand names for even wider sale.

There was both resistance and lack of interest. Traditional elite families initially stayed away, concerned that the stores were featuring unduly standardized goods for a debased mass taste, but ordinary people were hesitant also. Many were unaccustomed to leaving their particular neighborhoods for shopping. For both groups, the modernity of the new Ginza quarter, Tokyo's main department store center seemed intimidating and foreign. Stores such as Mitsukoshi made special efforts to woo the old aristocracy and members of the imperial household. They sponsored concerts and fashionable art shows as part of this campaign, going well beyond the activities of their Western counterparts. Other stores focussed more specifically on the lower and lower-middle classes, and by 1923 were pulling mass customers in with some regularity, aided by other innovations such as special sales as well as the ubiquitous advertising. By the 1930s, trips to department stores became tourist targets for people from rural districts; five percent of all customers emerged from this source. In 1932 a walking tour guidebook "for lovers" explained how a young couple could visit the "Five Great Department Stores" by subway. Clearly, the department stores had overcome earlier hesitation to become a leading vehicle for Japanese consumerism. Not surprisingly, branch outlets began to appear in other cities and towns.

Decades of reaction

The same decades that saw the rise of the great stores also saw a concerted government response, suggesting the same kind of oscillation about consumerism that occurred in China despite Japan's more eager commitment – or perhaps because of it. During the 1900s a new generation of government bureaucrats began to worry that the Japanese were not saving enough, as measured by the needs of what they called "national strength." Official campaigns for diligence and thrift urged, in the words of an Imperial Rescript of 1908, that people be "frugal in the management of their households . . . to abide by simplicity and avoid ostentation, and to inure themselves to arduous toil without yielding to any degree of indulgence." The campaign intensified during and after World War I. Officials attacked urban consumerism, terming it "luxury and self-indulgence." The new stores and movie houses spurred this kind of response, in the name of nationalism and a set of neo-Confucian values. References to "public-spiritedness" and a "spirit of self-sacrifice" abounded, in what was a major and sophisticated public advertising campaign. Moral Suasion Groups were founded to protect communities against the "winds of extravagance and habits of luxury," though the main targets were lower-class households that were instructed in careful household budgeting and savings. Trains, temples, and public buildings were blanketed with over two million posters in the mid-1920s.

This reaction went well beyond developments in the West, though Nazi Germany and fascist Italy offered some similarities. It played on some common themes, such as concern about the lower classes and preservation of social hierarchy; but the official embrace went well beyond Western norms.

On balance the campaign did not take full hold. Consumerism continued to advance, though savings rates went up as well. Doubtless different individuals reacted variously, and some experienced a tension amid their own expectations and goals. The campaign offers a fascinating window into the conflicts consumerism could generate, but in contrast to Chinese efforts its practical impact was muted. At most, the Japanese counterthrust prepared the population for the deprivations of World War II, when military necessity overtook consumerism amid widespread popular support.

The later twentieth century

Developments after World War II largely maintained the trajectories already established before the military interruption. Again, department stores led the way in expansion. Various stores tried to work up from a largely lower-class clientele, which raised image problems, or down from a more elite customer base. The Seibu group faced the drawbacks of a lower-class reputation, which it successfully combated by sponsoring major artistic exhibits and even setting up its own Museum of Art. Young and affluent buyers were drawn in on this basis. As in the West, many stores began to offer services as well as goods, but the range of commodities expanded as well. Key words in the postwar department store strategy clearly challenged more traditional Japanese culture: "lifestyle," "individualization" and "diversification." The lifestyle idea was imported from the United States, and focussed on identifying different groups, in terms of age, gender, and job, to whom different clusters of products would appeal as part of establishing identity. Advertising expanded, but in the same direction. Slogans included a "My Own Expression" series that highlighted a sense of self-centeredness and the idea of creating a "new self." Against ongoing traditions of conformity, Japanese consumerism successfully touted a decidedly individualistic stance – though as with Western individualism, this often meant buying the same products as did other members of one's group. As in Western malls, by the 1980s department stores of the classic type were beginning to yield to clusters of specialty shops – but this merely suggested another phase of consumerism, not a retreat.

Several developments were particularly noteworthy. Rural involvement increased greatly. Farmers viewed themselves as commercial actors, not peasants, and expected their work to be rewarded with telephones, television, and other consumer amenities. The government now supported the consumer trend, heralding "a new stage in consumer demand." By the 1950s and 1960s Japanese consumers referred to the three Ss as major life goals: *senpuki*, *sentakuki*, and *suihanki* (fan, washing machine, and electric rice cooker). But this soon yielded to three Cs, derived from words meaning car, air conditioner, and color TV, and then even three Js – jewels, jetting, and a house.

Many people used consumer gains to distinguish themselves not only from the poor, but from older generations. Traditional furniture yielded to more Western styles. Old family shrine alcoves in homes might be retained, but only because the new television sets fitted them. Home magazines pushed Western styles hard, as a symbol of modernity and healthy family life. High style served individual fulfillment but also a more rational approach to life generally. Japanese touches remained, however. Many people bought Western chairs but continued to prefer sitting on the floor.

The pressure of Americanization was extraordinary, the result both of United States leadership in global consumer standards and the experience of American postwar occupation. Competitions of housewives, sponsored by women's magazines, encouraged the use of a maximum number of American items, whose location in the home was facilitated by the American-imported family shows widely watched on television. American-style goods meant modernity but also a break from traditional obligations and hierarchy, toward greater individual self-determination.

The opening of Disney World in 1984 was a major consumer event. Japanese owners of the facility insisted that the American park in Los Angeles be duplicated as closely as possible – against American advice that more Japanese touches be added. A few modifications included a Westernland instead of Frontierland, for while American Westerns were familiar and touched base with a samurai-style, good guy over bad guy tradition, the frontier was not part of remembered Japanese experience. But the enthusiasm for access to American imagery was extraordinary. By 1988 over 13 million people visited annually, making the park one of the biggest leisure draws in Japan. Japanese familiarity with American icons such as Mickey Mouse derived from long experience with imported movies; the park seemed desirably American but also Japanese because of this shared tradition. And there were some explicit Japanese elements, including a movie called "Meet the World" that in fact highlighted Japanese identity in a global context. And, as always, even American items served national purposes. Buying gifts on Disneyland's Main Street – largely American items, but of better quality than in comparable outlets in the United States – served traditional gift-giving needs, not tourist nostalgia as in the United States. Japanese customs, called *sembetsu*, required a traveler to repay a farewell gift of money with a return gift from the location of the trip, with a tag or wrapper proving it was purchased on site. Since all Disneyland products were carefully stamped Tokyo Disneyland (again, a contrast to practice in the United States), the tradition was readily served in the seemingly Amercian context.

Even Christmas spread to Japan as an occasion for gift-giving, although the Japanese were not Christian. Ironically, the modern meaning of

Christmas in the commercial West proved more powerful than the religious meaning.

Japanese consumerism thus blended the national and the global, creating a mix that was as thoroughly consumerist as its Western counterpart without being fully Western. Some distinctive hesitations remained. Notably, despite widespread interest in consumer advance, late twentieth century Japanese continued to display much higher rates of personal savings than their Western, and particularly, American counterparts. Concerns for family security constrained consumerism more than in the West.

By the late twentieth century, indeed, Japan had become an international consumer leader in its own right. It could not rival the West in exporting standard styles. There was no Japanese equivalent to Hollywood, and the nation continued to import many of its consumer symbols, from fast foods to the Disney park. But the Japanese had become adept at producing consumer goods for global sales, often with significant innovations in technology and quality. Japanese products ranged from automobiles to electronic equipment, as the nation rose to the top rank of industrial powers. More subtly, certain Japanese creations had a style-setting capacity of their own. Japanese television cartoons were shown in many parts of the world. A Japanese soap opera, shown in translation in the Middle East, generated one of the most widely admired heroines in the region. Japanese toy design became the most creative in the world, though actual production increasingly centered in low-cost labor centers such as China. Overall, products designed for consumer enjoyment became the nation's largest export category by the early twenty-first century, partly because the Japanese themselves were setting a vigorous pace in consumer innovation. The American *Wired* magazine, in fact, selected young Japanese women as global trend setters, reporting on what they bought as probable models for wider consumer patterns later on.

Conclusion

The East Asian experience of consumerism suggests several conclusions. A few are obvious: consumerism has proved very attractive across national and cultural boundaries. Contact with the West in the nineteenth and twentieth centuries inevitably raised new expectations and also provided experience in the business apparatus consumerism involves. But different groups and even individuals reacted variously, and there were many signs both of reticence and of active opposition.

Overall, the East Asian context suggests some distinctive encouragements for consumerism, though also some constraints that differed from those in the West itself. Encouragement included the existence of strong consumer interests even before the nineteenth century as part of urban culture and a secular outlook. In these areas, East Asia contrasted interestingly with Russia, where urban values were less deeply rooted and where religious leadership was more prominent. It was noteworthy that religious objections to consumerism did not play a substantial role in the East Asian reaction. But traditions of social hierarchy and devotion to the public good, plus a strong attachment to customary styles, even for items such as household and dress, were genuine deterrents to the consumerist advance. There was also a strong commitment to cultural identity and to resistance to foreign interference. These traditions could feed newer objections, such as those emanating from Chinese communism.

In both China and Japan, the rise of consumerism represented a considerable change. It was impressive that, in both cases, consumerism became so closely associated with an almost fantasy-like modernity, and that some people would commit to aspects of consumerism – such as fast foods in China – that objectively they did not particularly enjoy, because of the larger symbolism involved. The strong individualist current in consumerism was also striking, as against more group-oriented traditions. This theme was deliberately played up in advertising, particularly in Japan, as if consumerism provided a larger release from customary hierarchies and constraints.

At the same time, again in both countries, consumerism did not triumph without concessions. Japanese interest grew steadily, but it was combined with a greater commitment to savings and group values. Both Japanese and Chinese merchants carefully combined the obvious appeal of Western styles with continued commitment to local craft output – some of which had considerable consumer potential of its own with the expansion of sales and markets. Finally, it was revealing that department stores in both countries emerged as cultural centers, beyond the scope of their Western progenitors, in sponsoring art, music, radio, and other activities associated with high culture and newer communications technologies alike.

The differences between the Chinese and Japanese experiences are also noteworthy. Japan did not deliberately pioneer in consumerism as part of its reform impulse, but consumerism proved fairly quickly to be part of the package – in contrast to obviously greater Chinese oscillations and long periods of outright resistance. China's firmer commitment to social and gender hierarchy played a role in hesitations. So, of course, did more widespread poverty, in a country deeply affected by rapidly rising population growth well before the nineteenth century. Consumerism was one of several phenomena that separated these two East Asian societies throughout most of the twentieth century, though by the century's end, given the striking rise of urban consumerism in China, the gap may have begun to narrow.

Further reading on China

Craig Clunas, *Superfluous Things: Material Culture and Social Status in Early Modern China* (Urbana: University of Illinois Press, 1991); Susan Naquin and Evelyn Rawski, *Chinese Society in the Eighteenth Century* (New Haven, CT: Yale University Press, 1987); Hen-p'ing Hao, *The Commercial Revolution in Nineteenth-Century China: The Rise of Sino-Western Mercantile Capitalism* (Berkeley, CA: University of California Press, 1986); Charlotte Ikels, *The Return of the God of Wealth: The Transition to a Market Economy in Urban China* (Stanford, CA: Stanford University Press, 1996); Linda Cooke Johnson, *Shanghai: from Market Town to Treaty Port, 1074–1858* (Stanford, CA: Stanford University Press, 1995); Leo Lee, *Shanghai Modern: The Flowering of a New Urban Culture in China, 1930–1945* (Cambridge, MA: Harvard University Press, 1999); Conghua Li, *China: The Consumer Revolution* (New York: J. Wiley & Sons, 1998); Dorothy Solinger, *Chinese Business under Socialism* (Berkeley, CA; London: University of California Press, 1984); Kerrie MacPherson, ed., *Asian Department Stores* (Richmond, Surrey: Curzon, 1998) (this also deals with Japan).

Further reading on Japan

Nishiyama Matsunosuke, *Edo Culture: Daily Life and Diversions in Urban Japan, 1600–1868* (Honolulu: University of Hawaii Press, 1997); Sharon Minichiello, *Japan's Competing Modernities: Issues in Culture and Democracy, 1900–1930* (Honolulu: University of Hawaii Press, 1998); Chia Nakane and Shinzaburo Oishi, *Tokugawa Japan: The Social and Economic Antecedents of Modern Japan* (Tokyo: University of Tokyo Press, 1990); Edward Seidensticker, *Low City, High City: Tokyo from Edo to the Earthquake* (Cambridge, MA: Harvard University Press, 1983); Joseph Tobin, *Re-made in Japan: Everyday Life and Consumer Taste in a Changing Society* (New Haven, CT: Yale University Press, 1992).

Chapter 9

Consumerism in Latin America

Substantial consumerism in Latin America was long delayed by extensive poverty. In 1800, for example, the average Mexican had a standard of living about two-thirds as high as a citizen of the United States. In 1900 this ratio had dropped to one-third. Americans had become more prosperous, and of course were engaging in increasingly elaborate consumer spending. But Mexicans had also become poorer, despite some industrial development at the end of the century.

For most Latin Americans, in fact, the chief connection to the rise of consumerism in the late eighteenth and nineteenth centuries was increasing involvement in low-wage production of goods for export. Latin Americans, in other words, fed consumerism elsewhere, mainly in Western Europe and the United States, without themselves having much access to it. It was in the nineteenth century, for example, that Brazil began to develop considerable coffee production – a low-wage, labor intensive cultivation that brought few rewards to the workers beyond bare subsistence. As with Africa, discussed in the next chapter, impoverishment made consumerism a non-topic for most people in this society. There was less precedent for consumerism than in East Asia, and pre-modern festivals had emphasized more collective celebration than individual display; cities remained smaller; and there was less overall economic opportunity as well.

One pattern did establish some directions for the future. A wealthy upper class of planters, a few merchants, and mine owners, enjoyed abundant means in the eighteenth and early nineteenth centuries. Like their counterparts in the United States South, they developed an elaborate lifestyle based substantially on imports from Europe, or on imitations of European fashions. Home furnishings, artwork, dress styles all followed the European model. Frequent travel to Europe reinforced the connections. Wealthy sections of cities such as Buenos Aires looked very much like equivalent parts of Paris or London. There was no objection, in this limited but influential circle, to consumerism, but a clear desire to define it in terms of keeping up with the Western elite.

This model of imitation would continue to guide much of Latin American consumerism in the twentieth century, when a somewhat larger urban middle class began to take shape. A middle-class consumer identity began to emerge, based heavily on patterns suggested by the United States.

Cuba provides a case in point. It opened increasingly to United States influence from 1900 onward. During the 1920s and 1930s, American retail chains, such as the big dime stores, spread widely in cities across the island. Department stores such as El Encanto were established. These developments transformed the act of shopping from a way to pass the time to a way to acquire goods. American magazines also gained a growing audience, particularly those providing cues for women. Many Cuban women saw particular opportunities in American-style consumerism, just as they were gaining new access to education and work roles – including, of course, roles as clerks in the new stores. Travel to the United States became common, and a critic noted that many women who returned from such visits were "too modern, maybe ultramodern."

By the 1940s, American dress styles so predominated in the Cuban middle classes that visitors were amazed at the elaborate clothing worn during intense summer heat. Even fur coats and wraps caught on. Undergarments, swimming suits, hats, cosmetics, and soaps – all followed North American fashion as a means of projecting success and status. American "experts" often visited department stores to guide Cubans in the latest ways to apply makeup or to "clarify whatever doubts you have with regard to the tones and models that correspond best to your figure" – this last from a representative of Catalina swimwear. American movies and popular music, including rock music by the 1950s, had wide audiences, and of course provided models of other consumer behavior.

The United States also provided leadership in home appliances and automobiles, most of which were imported directly. Not only in Cuba but also in Mexico and elsewhere, the growing middle class accounted for rapidly rising rates of refrigerator and television ownership.

Similar patterns also developed in South America. Brazil also saw a growing middle class by the 1920s, and the concomitant spread of American chain stores such as Sears, Roebuck. New urban residents, some of them involved in marginal clerical jobs, were eager to demonstrate some status by visible consumer spending. As in Cuba, by the 1920s many urban Brazilian women were wearing layers of French or American fashions, combined with makeup so heavy that it often ran in the heat. Advertisements appealed to the widespread quest for social recognition in a fluid urban environment. Ford Motors not only sold cars, but offered "true bumper to bumper modernism"; General Electric opened a store in 1932 with the theme: "modern homes . . . cannot fail to be in contact with General Electric Stores," while products such as refrigerators, radios, and toasters were "bound to increase the comfort and happiness of life." Critics complained that women were increasingly choosing men not on the basis of character or traditional values, but in terms of how many consumer goods they were likely to provide. Aspirations certainly ran high: one 1940s poll revealed that half of all homeowners said they needed a garage, even though less than twenty percent owned a car. Other observers argued that Brazil's middle classes so fully identified with consumerism that they neglected to develop any particular political allegiance or style.

In Brazil as in Cuba, rising consumerism frequently involved women, setting goals and pressing to establish a product-rich household and a fashionable appearance. Consumerism became wrapped up with new educational levels and work roles, part of a pattern of new assertiveness in a culture that had long emphasized women's subordination.

This kind of consumerism obviously had downsides – some quite familiar, many certainly shared with rising consumerism in places such as Africa. Criticism abounded. Many people complained about shallowness, about overturning established gender relations, about a loss of national identity to meaningless foreign models. Intellectuals hammered this latter theme, contending that a culture that had successfully fused European and native American values was now being replaced by a passion to resemble North America – a passion that could never in fact be realized, given the regional economic gap involved. Certainly many middle-class Latin Americans faced overwhelming tensions as they struggled to maintain a living standard many could barely afford. Interestingly, as in the United States, levels of consumer debt rose rapidly, a sign that goals were increasing more rapidly than means.

There were alternatives. The Cuban revolution in 1959 did not directly target consumerism. It was fueled, however, by groups too poor to participate in consumer pleasures, who resented the wealthier, foreign-oriented middle classes. It was fueled by middle-class people themselves, who were tired of the consumer rat race and who realized that their living standards (even when they were employed by United States corporations) lagged well behind North American levels, such that they were permanently caught between foreign aspirations and local constraints. And the communist regime did work to tone consumerism down, in part of course as ties to the United States were greatly curtailed. In 1961 the El Encanto department store burned down, in suspicious circumstances. The government helped transform Christmas away from the United States-style orgy of consumer gift giving, toward greater emphasis on traditional and Spanish rituals and goods. Overall, Fidel Castro's Cuba would emphasize collective loyalties, including military-style uniforms and impressive sports displays, over individual consumer standards.

Cuban communism proved to be an isolated case. More interesting was the Latin American ability both to maintain traditional styles alongside consumer interests, and to parlay some of these styles into consumer export items. Traditional festivals, such as Brazil's Carnival, not only held their own but gained increasing favor, an opportunity to show off customary fashions and rituals as well as imported beachwear. Latin American – particularly, Mexican – foods began to gain international favor after the 1950s. Even earlier, music and dance styles, from countries like Cuba, Argentina, and Brazil, spread widely, becoming part of fashionable global consumer culture. Between the 1920s and 1950s, mambos, sambas, and cha-cha-chas won large audiences; "Latin" themed clubs developed in most large United States cities; and bandleaders, particularly from Cuba, toured extensively in the West. This degree of mutual interaction with global consumerism helped reduce the foreign-ness of the phenomenon in Latin America itself.

By the end of the twentieth century, middle-class consumer culture in Latin America was not only well established. It had also shed some its most labored imitative qualities. Latin America participated with North America and Western Europe in increasingly informal and colorful fashions, often more appropriate to the climate. Signals were still accepted from the outside world. A classic consumer obligation for a middle-class family involved at least one outing to Disney World in Florida, complete with accumulation of souvenirs. But Latin American styles had their own international consumer market, which provided a certain degree of balance.

Great constraints still existed given the huge economic inequalities of Latin American society, both within major countries like Brazil, where consumer-oriented middle classes coexisted with impoverished street children, and from one region to the next. It was small wonder that religious interests, including widespread conversions to evangelical Protestantism, won new favor where consumerism was out of reach. Even the middle classes faced continued problems. Economic downturns, as in Argentina in the 1990s, could push large segments of the middle classes into real want. Consumerism was in this sense both limited and fragile. But the phenomenon now had Latin American roots; it was not simply an import. And aside from continued criticism by intellectuals, explicit hostility to consumerism, as opposed to the availability of cultural alternatives, was largely absent.

Further reading

Brian Owensby, *Intimate Ironies: Modernity and the Making of Middle-class Lives in Brazil* (Stanford, CA: Stanford University Press, 1999); Louis Pérez, Jr, *On Becoming Cuban: Identity, Nationality, and Culture* (Chapel Hill, NC: University of North Carolina Press, 1999); Maria Barber and Andrés Regalsky, eds, *Americanization, the United States, and Latin America in Century XX: Economic Transferences, Cultural Technologies* (Buenos Aires: National University Press, 2003); Fernando Rocchi, *La Americanización del Consumo: Las batallas por el Mercade Argentino, 1920–1945* (Buenos Aires: Universidad Tocuto Di Tella, 2003).

Chapter 10

Consumerism in Africa

African experiences with modern consumerism offer a number of distinctive features. Elements of consumerism, including interest in Western goods, go far back in African history, and while elites were particularly involved, ordinary people sometimes participated as well. While religion was vitally important in African life, there was no sweeping otherworldliness to complicate the response to consumer attractions in Africa below the Sahara, except to an extent in some Muslim centers. Nor was there an alternative value system such as Confucianism. Formal opposition to consumerism emerged slowly and incompletely. Africa had long been a peasant society, with vigorous emphases on family and community solidarity. Both widespread poverty and communal goals could limit consumer gains.

As in other societies, modern consumerism was closely associated with exposure to Western contacts, though there was a pre-Western market history in Africa as well. African use of foreign models, particularly in helping to define a new urban middle class, had some similarities with patterns in Latin America, but contacts were less systematic, with no overwhelming presence like that of the United States in countries such as pre-revolutionary Cuba. Intense interactions with the West came late in African history, and thus much of the story of modern consumerism is focussed on the late nineteenth century onward. This same period, however, saw increased economic exploitation of many Africans, limiting their consumer potential. As in most societies, economic and social divisions colored the response to consumerism, and increased attraction and growing misery coexisted in the African experience.

African consumerism, then, offers a chronology different from that of Russia or Asia. The pre-modern background suggests a potential eagerness for at least some consumer items that has distinctive qualities as well. African consumer history features a somewhat familiar set of divisions, for example between urban and rural, but less articulation of anti-consumer alternatives than was common elsewhere.

Before Imperialism

Sub-Saharan Africa boasted a lively merchant tradition dating back to the days of the great Sudanic kingdoms in West Africa, and to Swahili towns on the East African coast. Much of the trade was international, bringing African raw materials and slaves to the Middle East, and Middle Eastern or North African manufactured goods and horses in return; consumer items were not strongly featured. There were many local and regional markets, often staffed by women, that mixed necessities such as foods with brightly colored cloth and metal wares. Most Africans were rural, and traded infrequently if at all, but there was a vigorous urban tradition. There was also a strong sense of colorful style and self-presentation that supported early consumer interests and would feed modern consumerism later on.

New contacts with West European traders began in the fifteenth and sixteenth centuries. The most obvious result was the massive and terrible Atlantic slave trade, but African merchants sought products in return. Many European items came to be valued not because they were superior to African manufactures, but because of novelty value and style. Here, Africans differed from most Asians in the same period, who were not so attracted to Western wares. Thus European-made swords had special prestige, helping to define elite status. The same held true for cloth. African cloth won praise from Europeans – as one observer noted, "so beautiful that there is not better work done in Italy," but urban Africans, for example in present-day Ghana, developed a taste for imports, drawn by unusual colors and designs. European-made beads and jewelry offered similar attractions. Many were figured into works of art, as well as used in daily life. High-priced imports were valued in part because they were more expensive than more traditional, local adornments. A certain conspicuous consumption was involved here, a desire to be noticed; and it involved not only the rich and powerful but also successful traders, artisans, and commercial farmers. A German observer commented on an African interest in personal display. Thus one tribe, the Akan, were "so vain about what they wear – and whatever appeals to them at a particular time they must have, even if they have to pay twice as much for it."

Again, there are strong suggestions here of a potential consumerism less constrained than that in pre-modern East Asia. Perhaps Africa's lack of such firm social distinctions as Confucianism required opened individuals to this desire to make a mark through acquisition – much as in Europe during the eighteenth century, or as in the initial reactions of some Native American groups to European wares. Disapproval of individual expression was less strong than in Confucian culture, and elites complained less about innovative behaviors beneath them. There is also some indication that minor chiefs gained power not through inheritance but by the extent of their possessions, and this tradition could turn in consumerist directions as well.

The result was not, at this point in the seventeenth and eighteenth centuries, a high volume of consumer imports. Guns loomed larger in African purchases from Europe, but there was an impressive variety of items. As many as 150 different Dutch products, for example, showed up in West Africa, including forty different types of cloth. And demand often shifted, creating new fashions while rendering previous imports out of date and unsellable – another index of nascent consumerism. While most internal trade involved subsistence items, prestige goods gained ground as well, even among some ordinary Africans. Relatively humble people could contest what had been markers of status and political power, simply by expanding their range of acquisition.

Then came the end of the Atlantic slave trade, early in the nineteenth century, and a scramble to find alternative commercial exports, particularly through increasing the production of vegetable oils but also through growing trade in goods such as ivory. Many Africans were drawn into a low-wage commercial economy, or outright slavery within Africa, and obviously lost any clear consumer potential.

The impact of Imperialism, late nineteenth century to the 1950s

There were new inducements for consumerism as well. In the first place, contact with Westerners widened. Missionaries, for example, promoted use of Western-style clothing, for what they saw as decency rather than consumerism, but the result was the cultivation of new tastes. Missionaries also distributed free towels as an encouragement to hygiene, as well as religion, and this could open new interest in buying products for personal grooming. Western and Middle Eastern merchants also set up shops in some rural centers, offering a range of goods and increasing interest in consumer gains. Some Africans profited from commercial agriculture, winning new wealth and with it, new opportunities to demonstrate status by higher levels of consumption. Thus even some farmers gained access to new amounts of money, and sought imported cloth, beads or metal products as a reward for their production. European observers commented on how many East Africans not only enjoyed trade and barter, but also demonstrated a "willingness to change their customs" in order to acquire consumer goods. A similar openness was noted in West Africa in 1891. One group was described as

anxious to barter and quicker to trade and more eager for business than any natives I have yet seen. So keen are they on business . . . that they have broken up fresh ground and planted double crops this year, in order to supply the rush of white men.

This was a time of disruption, and consumer advances could provide identity and status as compensations.

For most of the new trade with Western Europe was not simply for
survival or for military needs. It still involved guns and horses, but also a
growing range of goods including "blankets, knives and cutlery, needles,
button, thread, crockery, pipes, snuff boxes, soap, sugar, even pictures and
umbrellas." And as ordinary Africans participated in new consumerism,
chiefs sought more rarified imports to preserve their distinctive status. Here,
the cachet of European manufacture loomed even larger. England, particularly, was seen as the source of particular prestige, and the result clearly
supported British imperialism. Again, the importance of social distinctions
but also a certain degree of social fluidity and rivalry fed the emergence of
fuller African consumerism, in a number of different coastal and urban
regions.

By the 1920s and 1930s, Western-style consumer interests were gaining
further ground. Many newly rich African merchants and farmers lived in
Western-style houses, and sported bicycles and Western art, and even an
occasional automobile. Migrant workers involved in commercial agriculture
or mining might be poorly paid, but they did earn some wages and they
sought new goods to spend them on. Western-style clothing and perfumes
drew attention, and even bicycles and sewing machines (which however
represented investments for greater production as well as consumer items).
A new urban class of clerks arose, working for Western businesses and
colonial governments, usually educated in Western-style schools. In Uganda
these mobile individuals were called "new people" because of their devotion
to modern products and their commitment to a Western-influenced urban
lifestyle.

For some of these new people, interest in consumerism could successfully
challenge older loyalties, a crucial and poignant test of how deeply the consumer interest ran. Nigerian author Chinua Achebe sets his story, revealingly
entitled "No Longer At Ease," in a 1920s Nigerian city. The protagonist
comes from a rural village, but is drawn into urban attractions involving more
open sexuality plus fashionable clothing and furnishings. In a crucial passage,
he learns of his mother's death, back in the village. Tradition insisted that
he should come home for the funeral but also for a prolonged stay to ensure
that family affairs are in order. But he holds back, sending some money
instead, because his new life could not be interrupted.

Other studies, focussing on the mid-twentieth century before independence, highlighted the extent to which many urban couples were willing to
work hard in the interests of buying more and better consumer products
for themselves and their children. Medicated and scented soaps gained
ground over customary washing techniques. Individual choice often predominated over traditional or communal standards. Commercial farmers began

to join the urban parade, building new houses with glass windows and wearing Western-style suits and ties. One observer suggested, among wealthier urbanites, a "revolutionary expansion" in the quest for durable consumer products, including radios and phonographs.

Women's interests might change, spurred in part by gains in literacy and the lures offered by popular magazines. Some bought African-American style hair products, and used commercial perfumes and hair dyes instead of traditional materials. European styles won great attention. A European observer claimed that "like European women, African women are very subject to influence points – one type of thing associated with Paris, another with America, another with Britain." A classic consumer story told of a young man who took his girlfriend with him to buy a shirt, but emerged instead with a blouse and two pairs of nylons for her. "I still don't know where I went wrong," the man lamented. And the advice-column answer was: "Lesson – never take your girlfriend into a shop when you have any money on you. Look the other way the minute you see anything for sale whenever she happens to be around."

But consumerism did not advance unchecked. Many African workers, and particularly rural people, resisted new ways. They viewed cities as "wildernesses" or "places for whites." If they worked for money, they viewed this as a temporary expedient to buy land or cattle and to permit marriage and a return to a fully agricultural life. Clearly, limited resources but also distinctive values constrained consumerism for the majority. In Achebe's story, the young urbanite is a frank consumer but his family roundly condemns his choices. "It was a thing of shame." "That is what the big city can do to a young man. He runs after sweet things, dances breast to breast with women and forgets his home and his people." "He was told that his mother died and he did not care. It is a strange and surprising thing."

Consumerism, in other words, was a central issue in a war between change and tradition, between the individual and intense communal and family ties. The battle was fierce in Africa because the majority of people remained rural. Further, women were far less likely to move to cities than men were, so despite the gibes about women's consumerism the gender qualities of the growing African consumerism leaned distinctively to the male side.

Finally, consumerism was partly foreign, at a time when resistance to European colonial controls was gaining momentum. As in many parts of Asia, consumer boycotts proved to be a common form of resistance. South Africans boycotted European merchants in 1921. West African cocoa farmers organized several boycotts in the 1920s and 1930s. The result was a clear demonstration that some things were more important than uninterrupted consumerism, in a society where consumerism itself was a fiercely-contested phenomenon.

Acceleration and new tensions since the 1940s

African consumerism had an important base before the continent was engulfed in European imperialism. Further contact with the West expanded this base, though amid important tensions with more traditional values, and particularly family obligations. During the past half-century, sub-Saharan Africa witnessed an intensification of economic exploitation, but also the rise of new independence movements and finally independence itself. These larger events inevitably affected the development of consumerism, along with consumerism's own internal dynamic.

In fact, during the past fifty years, there have been three intertwined stories concerning Africans' engagement with consumerism. The first and most predictable is intensification. More Africans became acquainted with consumerism, more found meaning in it. The greater involvement of women was an important aspect of this. This theme also embraced the arrival of more sophisticated consumer apparatus, including larger stores and more formal advertisement.

The second story involves ongoing tension with older loyalties. Many Africans shunned consumerism. Growing poverty played a role here; the twentieth century has not been kind to the African economy, either before or after political independence. While cities have grown rapidly, the majority of the population remains rural, and rural Africans have often either ignored or positively rejected many of the trappings of consumerism. In many parts of the subcontinent, disease – the spread of AIDS but also malaria – periodic famines, and displacement in civil wars continue to create a struggle simply to survive; consumerism is irrelevant in this situation, not even a distant dream.

The third story involves the complicated relationship between consumerism, white racial attitudes, and African reactions. Europeans both promoted and resisted African consumerism. Even as they promoted it, they often incorporated offensive racial assumptions. Africans often held back from consumerism because of the racial connotations (though some plunged on). More commonly, they worked to give their participation in consumerism their own meanings.

The acceleration process has involved a number of facets. Consumerism in Africa lagged behind developments in many other parts of the world, but it began to demonstrate much the same dynamic. Rural stores, or what was called the "truck" trade, spread further, often trading consumer goods for agricultural products. Clothing and ornaments were the most popular items, followed by tools and then patent medicines and soaps, with cigarettes and bicycles next on the list. Then in the 1960s and 1970s, larger urban stores opened (in southern Africa, department stores had emerged earlier, but mainly for whites). Chain stores and other outlets such as *Kumboyedza* and *Jazz* sprang up in African shopping districts in the cities, with all the usual apparatus of mass distribution. Producers, not only in

Europe but also in Japan and India, were by this point making cheap consumer goods expressly for the African market. Other products, such as the new soaps, were manufactured in African regions, though by foreign firms. Intriguingly, a large market also developed for second-hand Western clothing. The development mirrored what had happened in Europe in the eighteenth century, when consumerism also began to soar, but here it was defined also in terms of a quest for foreign, Western cachet. Africans gave the imported second-hand items many different names, such as *Vietnam* in Zaire, *calamidades* in Mozambique, or a local name that means "dead white men's clothes" in Ghana. Buying Western used clothing was not a simple attempt to become Western, but it did give African consumers a sense of being part of a larger global world – a gain similar to what participation in other forms of consumerism offered many East Asians.

The interest in consumerism for status continued. East Africans called newly-rich merchants *"wa-benzi,"* because of their devotion to Mercedes-Benz cars.

Intensified consumerism continued to mean novelty and change to the Africans and consumer agents alike. A white advertiser in South Africa made the point clearly, from the seller's side, in 1960. J.E. Maroun argued that marketing did not exist to satisfy consumers, but to

> create needs, sell solutions to problems, make people desire what you have to sell . . . From the outset, we must realize that almost all our efforts in the African market should be designed predominantly to change culture – the traditional way of doing things – and in some instances even to introduce ideas which are foreign to and contradict tradition and, therefore, will meet with resistance . . . We are offering the African new solutions to his problems and in many cases even new problems.

Africans themselves saw new acquisitions in terms of change. Many women began to migrate to cities expressly to obtain new goods, which would in turn give them a new identity and meaning.

> There was a sense of freedom about staying on your own in Johannesburg, and things like furniture we had seen others bring as fruits of their work in the towns urged us to follow suit. We had all seen our older sisters returning from such towns with beautiful dresses, shoes, plates, cups and at times they would have lighter complexions too.

Even in the countryside, women could often barter foods for new goods, particularly when their husbands were away working in the mines or the cities, though the result, one observer said, was "quite a lot of unpleasantness between husband and wife." As in other societies, goods were valued in their own right and also for the dreams they could inspire. A woman gets some money for selling grain. She

> gazed around the store, drinking in the pleasure of anticipated purchase . . . the woman gingerly fingered the top of a blanket, slowly unfolding it. She seemed torn between the attraction of the broad red stripe on one and the triple green ditto on the second . . . The prospective buyer turned the green-banded blanket over and over, feeling its texture.

Here was new consumerism in its most classic form.

Advertising increased. By the 1970s African beauty pageants were gaining ground, a clear innovation. To launch a new detergent in 1969, a marketing firm in Zimbabwe used a helicopter to drop leaflets over villages, periodically landing so that "Mr. Power-Foam," a black weightlifter, could disembark and distribute free samples. Increasing numbers of European and American firms set up African branches, in areas such as hygiene products and cosmetics.

But of course not everyone was drawn in. The new rural stores often drew criticism for high prices and unfair sales pressures. When the owners were European, Middle Eastern, or Indian, the tensions could involve a racial clash as well. Many people, men and women alike, worked not for consumer goods, but to acquire land; if they succeeded, they pulled away from labor for pay. A Kenyan woman in the 1970s described her life goals to an anthropologist. No pure traditionalist, she wanted more education for women and a lower birth rate, and she wanted women to organize commercial sales for the goods they produced. But her goal was family solidarity in a new context, not a consumerist heaven; acquiring new goods did not enter into the discussion at all.

The result of growing consumerism and continued resistance was a series of quiet dilemmas. Urban Africans often described how they were pulled between old goals and new. They wanted to improve the standard of living for their families and use acquisition to demonstrate their modernity, but villagers insisted on stopping by when they came to town, and tradition held that the host family owed them hospitality – even though the cost might erode any possibility of consumer gain. Some families honored tradition, others pulled away in resentment; either way, it was hard to feel good about the process. Other tensions might involve deciding between a traditional dowry, often measured in numbers of livestock available, and more urban consumer goods, when launching a marriage. The dilemmas were intense. Newspaper advice columns carried frequent laments.

> Though I have a good job I am kept poor by home-people. I go without the decent clothes my position calls for. I do not dislike the home-people, but what can I do to be saved from them?

While there was no sweeping anti-consumerist movement in Africa – again, an important distinction as consumerism gained ground – consumerism did enter a larger debate about what it meant to be African. Part of the debate was framed by white colonial administrators and business people in Africa. As early as the 1930s, many colonial regimes began to promote consumerism directly, realizing that if they changed African habits sales would go up. An official in Rhodesia (now Zimbabwe) noted that:

> as long as the natives have no wants they will not and need not work . . . Create for him as many wants as possible and induce him to adopt more modern methods of cultivation and tear him away from his beer pots.

In this view, a key purpose for education was to inculcate new needs, for better furnishings, utensils, and dress. And of course there was a decided movement toward more European-style items for personal adornment and for the home.

White settlers simultaneously worried about this same process. If Africans adopted Western style, they might also want new rights. Africans who dressed like Westerners were often described as "cheeky" or "arrogant." The debate was very similar to earlier criticisms of working-class consumerism, though in Africa it had an explicitly racial tinge. Africans were criticized for wasting money on items they did not need. Their expropriation of European styles showed their growing lack of proper deference. A missionary handbook tried to argue that Africans hurt their bodies by covering them with clothes: "the natural (naked) body is more able to resist disease than the thickly clothed one of the European."

> To the African, the wearing of a hat serves no useful purpose . . . it is to them an unnecessary expense only. As a rule, Africans do not understand the use of hats; they wear them anywhere and everywhere; in the night, outside as well as inside the house; and they wear them especially if they wish to make a show.

Some white business people sought to deal with the problem by selling "African-only" goods – consumer items, but different in style and particularly in quality from what Europeans had. But this strategy had only limited success. As Africans gained greater independence from colonial control, the most overt racism lost some force.

A related if more subtle problem persisted even after formal colonialism ended. While explicit "Africa-only" products receded, many producers continued to imbue their offerings, and their advertising, with racist assumptions. Soaps and cosmetics provide a key example, as their range expanded from the 1950s onward. Many soaps were powerfully scented to deal with what European colonists believed to be a special problem with African odor. Great emphasis was also placed on skin whiteners, and some Africans unquestionably welcomed these products. As one ad noted, "Ambi can give you the smooth, clear, lighter skin you've noticed successful people usually have . . . " While advertising began to take on more race-blind qualities by the 1970s, there were some lingering distinctions still. Some advertisements for example emphasized improving work ability, which touched base with European prejudices about African laziness. ("I'm glad . . . I'm feeling better. And the boss is pleased, too.") Soaps were offered particularly to men, with the implication that they would help men meet the social rules of a white-controlled workplace. More generally, advertisements urged the importance of products in order to appear middle-class and "smart" – that is, modern and sophisticated, part of a social world of comfort and power.

African response to these pitches was mixed. Some, obviously, bought into the message, wanting to look and feel more Western. Others, however, criticized the foreign tone and its patronizing implications. Nationalist intellectuals objected to the inroads on African values, arguing that transposing Western advertising techniques into regional languages either lacked meaning or caused severe cultural dislocation. Stores themselves might be regarded with suspicion, because of their strangeness and their insistent marketing. Advertisements also were carefully assessed, by ordinary folk as well as nationalist skeptics. An old villager, for example, remembers when posters went up claiming that "Coke adds life." He knew this was wrong, because he felt no extra energy after he drank a Coke to test the claim. The sense of fraudulent manipulation ran strong.

A few leaders urged government action, for example to ban imports of second-hand clothing. This provoked heated debate in Zambia in the 1990s, but few governments tried to interfere. Even African Marxists held back from sweeping attacks. Africa simply did not generate the period of government anti-consumerist action experienced by Japan and China.

The divisions in African reactions to consumerism were not uncommon, as they ranged from eager embrace to deep suspicion or avoidance. In between, many Africans sought to put their own mark on the phenomenon. Even the process of buying imported second-hand clothes allowed individual choices about the mixture of Western and African, about the selection of particular items. Consumerism and identity are always complexly linked. In a society where identity had been battered by over a century of intense Western interference, the preoccupation with taking charge of consumerism was particularly important. More than in some societies, the preoccupation was also highly individual, for there were no sweeping cultural movements or government measures to guide the process. Even used Western clothing could be redefined as new and African in this endeavor.

Further reading

Pre-Independence: T.L.V. Blair, *Africa, A Market Profile* (London: Business Publications Limited, 1965); Ian Phimister, *An Economic and Social History of Zimbabwe, 1890–1948* (New York: Longman, 1988); Peter Delius, *A Lion Amongst the Cattle: Reconstruction and Resistance in the Northern Transvaal* (Oxford: J. Currey, 1996); Jonathon Glassman, *Feasts and Riot: Revelry, Rebellion, and Popular Consciousness on the Swahili Coast, 1856–1888* (Portsmouth, NH: Heinemann; London: James Currey; Nairobi: E.A.E.P.; Dar es Salaam: Mkuki Na Nyota, 1995); A. Adu Boahen, *African Perspectives on Colonialism* (Baltimore, MD: Johns Hopkins University Press, 1987); John Thornton, *Africa and Africans in the Making of the Atlantic World, 1400–1680* (Cambridge; New York: Cambridge University Press, 1995).

More recent developments: Timothy Burke, *Lifebuoy Men, Lux Women: Commodification, Consumption and Cleanliness in Modern Zimbabwe* (London: Leicester University Press, 1996); Philip Bonner, Isabel Hofmeyr, Deborah James, and Tom Lodge, *Holding their Ground: Class, Locality and Culture in 19th and 20th Century South Africa* (Johannesburg, South Africa: Witwatersrand University Press; Braamfontein, Johannesburg: Raven Press, 1989); Belinda Bozzoli, *Women of Phokeng: Consciousness, Life Strategy and Migrancy in South Africa, 1900–1983* (Johannesburg: Raven Press, 1991); Karen Hansen, *Salaula: The World of Secondhand Clothing and Zambia* (Chicago: University of Chicago Press, 2000).

Chapter 11

Consumerism in the Islamic Middle East

Like East Asia and Africa, the Middle East had a proud tradition of urbanism and merchant activity, both of which could prefigure a fuller commitment to consumerism. For many centuries, indeed, Islamic merchants from the Middle East had led the world in trade. Market activity was a prominent and cherished part of city life, though of course the majority of the population remained rural. Many people enjoyed the process of shopping, picking out new items and haggling over prices. Elites delighted in ornate furnishings and jewelry, and artisanal products for consumption could rival those of any other region in the world. Many consumer items were enjoyed privately, in the seclusion of the home, particularly where women were involved.

But the Middle East offered another distinctive feature, in its general commitment to the powerful religion of Islam. Here is a clear contrast with other cases we have examined. In the West, consumerism rose among powerful strains of Christianity, but in an atmosphere where religious intensity, on the whole, was in decline. China and Japan had important religions but the dominant value systems, based on Confucianism, were secular. African religious commitment ran high, but there was no single religious system. The interaction between Islam and consumerism thus represents a distinctive interplay between powerful, ongoing spiritual values and the new lures of consumerism.

Islam was by no means hostile to material display. It did not attack wealth, so long as the rich paid their due to charity. It did not emphasize the holiness of material denial as much as traditional Christianity or Buddhism did, but it certainly put spiritual obligations first. And there were other potential constraints. The customs that had grown up around women in the Islamic Middle East, involving sober costumes and veiling, did not encourage public consumer display in the female sex (though there was considerable traditional interest, where means allowed, in jewelry). Islam and modern consumerism, in other words, were going to be somewhat uneasy partners at best, and could readily move to a collision course. Islam also offered a pride in traditional identities that could easily disparage imported standards, particularly from the infidel West.

The response to consumerism in the Islamic Middle East has been varied, among different groups and specific countries. Divided reactions are in fact one of the most important results of consumerist pressures in this complex region. Even reformers, for example in Turkey, shied away from a full embrace of consumerism, and some of the most vivid recent upheavals, such as the Iranian revolution, targeted consumerism as one of the chief enemies of Islamic purity.

This chapter looks at reactions, particularly during the twentieth century, in the Middle East and North Africa, which constitute the heartland of Islam. It is important to remember, of course, that Islam also commands loyalties in many other regions, such as South East Asia, where reactions to consumerism have often taken a rather different course.

Backdrop

Long before the economic advance of Western Europe, the Middle East was a center for the production of and trade in consumer goods. Cities featured bazaars, or *suqs*, in which concentrations of artisans made a variety of products. Some, of course, were for ordinary daily life or for religious use, but most larger towns also specialized in certain superior craft goods that were traded over wide areas. Fancy cloth (for wear but also for table decoration), elaborate metalwork, glassware, soap, and jewelry fell into this category, destined primarily of course for purchase by a wealthy minority. Some cloths even took their names from the place of origin, such as muslins from Mosul or damask from Damascus. Furthermore, imports, such as silks and porcelain from China and spices from South Asia, added to the consumer array. Wealthy Middle Easterners imported tea and sugar long before these items began to gain popularity in Europe.

Imports from Western Europe began to supplement the consumer array by the sixteenth century. European merchants had a particular motivation to win Middle Eastern sales, because they were eager to obtain Middle Eastern spices and luxury products and needed to be able to pay for these desired imports through successful exports. European cloth quickly gained a foothold – British and French woolens plus Italian fabrics. Some of this was crude and cheap, but more expensive items appealed to the new aristocracy of the Ottoman Empire. Interestingly, European merchants, particularly the French and Italians, quickly gained skill at determining local taste preferences, carefully reporting to production centers back in Europe so that the latest enthusiasms could be exploited. There was no consumer revolution here: local goods continued to predominate, and most people were not consumerist by any stretch of the imagination. But among some Middle Eastern elites, pride in having the latest European item began to be added to the attributes of high status. By the eighteenth century, Bohemian glass and Swiss watches fell into this must-have category among well-placed Turks in Istanbul. French cloth was used for festivals, when, as a British observer claimed, "everyone who can afford it must have a new set of clothes" for themselves and their servants.

Western consumer influence increased steadily during the nineteenth century, because of the outpouring of factory goods from Europe combined with new transportation systems, notably the railroad, that facilitated penetration, and the advent of outright European imperial regimes particularly in North Africa. Western-controlled imports of coffee and tea, and particularly the ubiquitous pressure in textiles, changed the balance of trade significantly. Regional production declined in many cases. British textile exports to the Middle East quintupled between the 1820s and the 1840s, by which time an average of four yards of British cloth per person were being sold. In a culturally diverse region, many ethnic minorities (including Christians) found meaning in adopting Western styles, as a way to demonstrate an identity separate from the Muslim majority. Nevertheless, emphasis on occasional decorative objects, such as jewelry boxes and clocks, predominated over clothing, suggesting some real limits on the Western consumerist influences.

There was also resistance to European consumer leadership. Many traditionalists preferred locally produced clothing, which the Europeans could not imitate precisely. There was also hostility to growing European political and military influence that could be expressed by refusing to buy foreign consumer items. Finally, there was outright opposition, based on a combination of political and religious factors. The Ottoman sultan issued several edicts during the eighteenth century against Western goods, mainly in a vain attempt to protect the regional economy against excessive imports. A 1758 imperial decree blasted "Frankish-style dress"(using a term that dated back to the crusades), noting that the "harm and inauspiciousness of this abominable state of affairs was . . . the cause of the disturbance of the order and regulation of subjects." In 1759–1760, another edict forbade women from wearing "extravagant clothing" in public markets, invoking the Qu'ran in insisting on simplicity and modesty in dress. The capacity to venture this kind of explicit objection declined in the nineteenth century, along with the diminution of Ottoman political power. But the hesitation persisted, particularly among Muslims. Along with extensive, often growing poverty and the gap between the rural majority and urban life, these factors inhibited the growth of a really new consumer spirit, even amid substantial changes in the economic balance of power.

Signs of change and resistance

The pace of change began to accelerate in the 1890s, particularly in major cities such as Istanbul. Western firms and imitative local operations were both involved. Consumer advertisements emerged in Arabic and Turkish, for products such as Singer sewing machines. The approach was cautious, for the new objects were depicted in carefully traditional settings; thus the sewing machine sat on an ornate ironwork table atop a Turkish-style rug. The idea of dramatic breakthroughs to modernization was downplayed in favor of a more syncretic framework. The same blending occurred in marketing. Few department stores emerged. Rather, new techniques and items were inserted in the customary urban bazaars. Products began to be highlighted for low cost and ease of purchase and new credit arrangements were introduced. The Herdjai Store in the famous Istanbul covered markets offered jewelry, canes, and watches (from cheap to quite expensive) on terms of five percent payment per week (while shoppers paying in cash received a five percent discount). Despite laws forbidding Muslim women from shopping in non-Muslim stores, women began to appreciate the new shopping experience. A suburban woman described her first experience: "The cleanliness, good nature, and organization in this store is magnificent, and the courteous treatment and honorable behavior truly dazzle the eyes." As in other cases of new consumerism, far more was involved than distinctive acquisition alone. Shopping could open new horizons and challenge established relationships.

In comparison to developments in cities such as Tokyo or Shanghai in the same period, change was surrounded by hesitations. Few advertisers broke through Muslim prohibitions against representing the human form, even to feature clothing, unless the person depicted was clearly a Westerner. A few venturesome merchants suggested outright Western styles, both for men and women. In one case, a veiled woman was shown shopping in a fashionable Paris-type clothing store, and a few Muslim women were venturing into such spots, but this was rare. There were more satirical criticisms of women's defiance than real innovation. Similarly, while a few stores touted the fact that their goods were imported – for example, silk fabrics – many others combined new sales pitches with an emphasis on regionally made goods, even when modeled after Western standards. Cigarette advertisements in Egypt, though particularly targeting a growing urban lower middle class of office clerks, alternated between appealing to a Western-style modernism, and associating cigarettes with more traditional settings; only a few evoked women smoking. A nationalistic, anti-foreign impulse combined with new consumer interests in complex ways.

The fact remained, however, that by 1900 up-to-date styles in ready-made clothing were available for urban Muslims. And Ottoman officials, posing for family photographs, might choose Western suits and dresses (with no veils for women), just as their analogs in Japan had been doing since the 1880s. New smoking habits spread as well.

Clearly, many of the same pressures visible in East Asia were beginning to affect turn-of-the-century Islam, in the leading urban centers. Western example and local desire to break away from sheer tradition, even in the experience of shopping, were beginning to be contagious. The tentativeness, compared to East Asia, remained impressive, as Islam and nationalism combined to affect the speed of change and the ways innovation was presented.

The twentieth century: new divisions

Shifts in the larger framework of Middle-Eastern society after 1918 opened the door for more extensive developments, though the constraints persisted as well. The collapse of the Ottoman Empire removed the remnants of strong government in the region as a whole. The kind of political buffer against consumerism that had operated under the sultans' guidance was drastically reduced for several decades. Middle Eastern governments were not strong enough to rival the anti-consumerist political measures of East Asia during the middle decades of the century. At the same time, Western influence increased even aside from the new international commercial outreach of eager exporters. European administrations took control over countries such as Syria and Lebanon. One key government, the new regime in Turkey, avoided neo-colonialism but began to impose its own active Westernization, which included attack on a number of Muslim habits (such as traditional clothing) with significant consumerist implications. Finally, Western economic penetration accelerated dramatically in pursuit of oil. Many Middle Easterners could now witness Western leisure and consumer habits directly, through the growing Western colonies dotting not only the big cities, but also the oil regions.

These various changes, taking shape after 1918 and often intensifying with time, created new opportunities for abrupt conversions to Western-type consumer norms. The change was vivid in the case of many women, who began to opt for Western dress and cosmetics against regional traditions. Consumer interests began to spread more widely, but there were important hesitations compared to East Asia or sub-Saharan Africa. The changes that did occur, plus foreign involvement, could provoke new kinds of resistance, and this became increasingly obvious in the final decades of the twentieth century. Consumerism divided Middle Eastern society; it even divided many individuals to some extent, torn as they were between two different value systems. The rifts remained wide at the outset of the twenty-first century.

The most striking changes in context were political. Turkey and then Iran featured new regimes that worked vigorously for various kinds of modernization, in the 1920s and 1930s. Their efforts included both attacks on traditional habits and selective encouragement for new types of consumer behavior. In Turkey, the nationalist leader, Kemal Attaturk, moved against customary Muslim clothing styles for both men and women. For example, he banned the fez, the traditional male headgear, and urged conversion to the Western-style hat.

It was necessary to abolish the fez, which sat on our heads as a sign of ignorance, of fanaticism, of hatred to progress and civilization, and to adopt in its place the hat, the customary head-dress of the whole civilized world, thus showing that . . . no difference existed between the Turkish nation and the whole family of civilized mankind.

The government also argued against veiling for women, and encouraged adoption of Western dress; this opened the door to additional kinds of purchases, such as cosmetics. The same pattern emerged in Iran in the 1930s, where the government sent women speakers to girls' schools to explain the benefits of European dress. After the veil was banned in Iran, policemen tore chadors or scarves away from women who appeared veiled on the streets. While a number of women stayed home as a result, feeling that being unveiled in public was a form of undress, most women had to appear in public in what was often an odd assortment of Western clothes.

Reformist regimes also promoted consumer industries in the home country. The goal here was not so much to encourage consumerism but to protect a fragile industrial economy against floods of imports; but the effect could nevertheless promote consumer interests. Among other things, production of Western-style clothing increased.

The resultant changes were real. Many people were forced away from established habits in ways that could stimulate a new desire to base a modern identity on novel, and Western-style, acquisitions. Nevertheless, a variety of impressive limitations persisted.

In the first place, few regimes matched the reformism of Turkey and Iran. French and British colonial administrations in Arab regions were far more hesitant, lest they promote political opposition. We will see that the French, for example, constrained the expansion of Western films. A number of independent Arab regimes, notably Saudi Arabia, continued to enforce customary behaviors, particularly where clothing (and more particularly, women's clothing) was concerned. Even in Turkey and Iran, change was slow and uneven. In Iran, Muslim-run girls' schools, even when headed by women, often turned away the government speakers who wanted to promote new clothing styles, and the speakers could enter only when backed by police escorts. The Muslim clergy actively preached against change.

Poverty was another limit. Civil servants often wrote to the Iranian government asking for financial assistance to buy Western-style clothes for their wives, arguing that they could not afford the change on their own.

Most important, lots of people simply did not want to change. Even when compulsion forced adjustments, the spirit behind choices of styles remained unaltered, and consumerism did not emerge. A key case involved rural men in Turkey, still the vast majority of men overall. The government did force them to abandon the traditional baggy pants, vests, and jackets of the Ottoman past, for Western garb. But the result was a conversion to the sack coats popular in Europe and the United States before World War I, which were quickly incorporated in a static rural culture. Village men remained identifiable into the 1970s because they had no interest in keeping up with changes in style.

Finally, even the policy of import substitution had its drawbacks from the consumerist standpoint. Locally produced goods might not be widely available (a problem in other developing countries such as the Soviet Union), and the quality might be poor. As late as the 1990s, for example, a high-ranking Turkish government official was reported to have told the president of the Automotive Manufacturers' Association: "Your cars are crap. I will recommend Mercedes as my preference for the official car purchases." Furthermore, governments themselves held back from full endorsement of consumerism, because they were eager to reserve funds for industrial and military investment and because they shared some of the cultural anxiety about change. Kemal Attaturk thus often scolded urban women in Turkey who seemed to be moving too fast toward Western styles, arguing that their behaviors were selfish and risked wasting money and damaging the family.

The combination of tentativeness and real change showed clearly in the emergence of movies in the 1920s and 1930s in countries such as Syria and Lebanon. Movies began to spread rapidly after World War I, showing mainly French, English, and American fare. By 1922 cities such as Damascus and Beirut had three or four movie houses, but the genre did not catch on too widely. The movies were located in less respectable areas, alongside cafes and music halls that catered to traveling merchants and minorities, rather than the Muslim majority. They were also often owned by foreigners or non-Muslims.

Once the era of silent films ended, the foreign language speech limited the clientele to elites who could speak English or French, for the audience was too small to justify the use of Arabic subtitles; and costs were too great for locally produced films in any number, until well after World War II. (Only in Egypt, after 1932, did any significant Arabic film industry emerge, and imports to the rest of the region were limited until later, partly because the costs of movie attendance were too high for most urban families.) Furthermore, the Western movies that were shown quickly drew moral protest, from Muslim but also Christian and Jewish leaders. It is important to note that similar attacks developed in the United States, against sexual immorality; but the resonance was greater in the Middle East. Thus many Muslim leaders argued that women should be banned from theaters alto-gether. Ordinary Muslims often agreed. Students sometimes disrupted movies that they viewed as immoral, setting off stink bombs to drive the audience out. In 1932 several hundred men in Lebanon petitioned the government to ban all women from any entertainment hall. Colonial admin-istrations varied in their responses, but they too often supported censorship drives. The French were eager to assure Muslims that Europe was not immoral and corrupt, as they approved film censorship in the 1930s.

Interest in movies grew steadily nonetheless, and with it some broader awareness of Western consumer standards. Boys often climbed to apartment roofs to watch open-air movies. Most upper- and middle-class urban women had attended at least one movie by 1930, and some fell in love with the genre. Nadida Shaykh al-Ard, in Damascus, later a feminist advocate for unveiling, recalled skipping classes to attend Gary Cooper movies with her friends. While some students backed Muslim censorship, others protested that movies were "a means of instruction in civilization." A Beirut student movement in 1931 also attacked high taxes on tickets, urging wider access. By 1939, 44,000 movie tickets were being sold per week in Syria and Lebanon, suggesting a substantial urban audience. And the cultural impact could be seen as wider still. In 1946 a future historian, Albert Hourani, wrote in Lebanon:

> the patriarchal family remains in existence, but its days are probably numbered. The process of change is being speeded by one manifestation of Western civilization above all: the film which expresses a way of feminine life, and a conception of relations between men and women, which are far from those prevalent in the Islamic world.

Of course the pace of change tended to accelerate after World War II, based in part on the new interests that had surfaced, however hesitantly, in the prior decades. The size of the urban middle classes grew in countries such as Turkey and Egypt, and with this came both money and motivation to expand consumer purchases. Both local production and imports of consumer goods expanded. By the 1990s, for example, Turks were buying 200,000 new cars a year, a marked increase from the previous 65,000 average. The arrival of television added not only another consumer item, but also wider access to consumer values more generally. Movies had advertised a few products, such as cigarettes and cars, but television expanded the range considerably.

Television arrived in Iran in the 1970s, with the first commercial station run by an American. Advertising emphasized clothing and cosmetics for women and the growing array of household appliances such as refrigerators and vacuum cleaners. The key market involved status-conscious housewives. Numbers of viewers expanded steadily, from 2.1 million around 1970 to 15 million, half the Iranian population, by 1974. Most of the programming involved serials and movies imported from the United States (taking up over half the broadcasting time). Clearly, an increasingly eager consumerist impulse was emerging among middle-class urbanites, anxious to keep pace with the latest trends in acquisition, as the basis for maintaining a "modern" home.

Even in conservative countries such as Saudi Arabia, increasing interaction with the West plus the surge in oil revenues created new levels of wealth that sought consumerist outlets. Massive shopping sprees in Western stores and commitments to expensive habits such as luxury automobiles, suggested the power of consumerism even when strong commitments to tradition and to Islam persisted.

Many people in the Middle East were clearly participating in the kind of consumerist involvements that had affected other parts of the world during the modern centuries. The pace had been a bit slower than, for example, in East Asia, but many of the directions seemed similar. And the fact of hesitation and opposition was not unique to the Middle East; it is important not to overdo the contrasts.

Still, however, many developments remained double-edged. Advances of consumerism in Iran, for example, brought loud protests not only from traditionalists but also from nationalists, often in the middle class itself, who continued to see the emblems of consumption as foreign, without connection to the regional culture. The advance of commercial television drew some into greater awareness of consumer attractions, but showed others how repulsive consumerism could appear. Advertising taught rural and working-class viewers about the gulf in wealth and attitudes between a limited, cosmopolitan upper class and the bulk of the Iranian population. Mixed sentiments of envy and outrage, of cultural inferiority and cultural pollution, grew among the traditional majority. Here was a context in which, even toward the end of the twentieth century, an astonishing anti-consumerist outcry could still emerge.

Both the power and the tremendous limitations of change emerged in a new Islamic attack on consumerism. Anti-consumerism, and of course related hostility to Western materialistic influence, were integral parts of the rise of Islamic fundamentalism from the 1970s onward. Here, indeed, was the most vivid recent attack on consumerism overall, anywhere in the world, and one of the most sweeping reactions ever experienced in consumerism's world history.

A number of factors provoked Islamic fundamentalism, and key outcroppings such as the Iranian revolution in 1979, but the reassertion of traditional culture against superficial, commercial Western products was central. Muslim leaders, such as the Ayatollah Khomeini in Iran, rose against foreign-inspired secularism. Rural and lower class urban residents attacked the urban middle class, using consumerism as a target for larger resentments against new privilege and inequality.

Khomeini had blasted the Western consumer orientation of Iran's government, including of course its abolition of the veiling of women (in 1938), as early as the 1940s. He claimed that urbanites "were strolling up and down the streets with a chamber-pot shaped hat, were occupied with naked girls," not realizing that Westerners were laughing at the awkward imitations even as they took commercial profits out of the region. Needless to say, Khomeini's attack simply increased as the Iranian revolution unfolded.

"We have nothing to say to those whose powers of perception are so limited that they regard the wearing of European hats, the cast-offs of the wild beasts of Europe, as a sign of national progress." The targets were clear: all those "who have grown up with lechery, treachery, music and dancing, and a thousand other varieties of corruption," who "regard the civilization and advancement of the country as dependent upon women's going naked in the streets." "It is a veritable flood of forbidden consumption that sweeps past us, right before our eyes."

What was needed was a religious crusade, a jihad, against the new materialism. Islam itself provided the touchstone, in its commitment to simplicity and modesty. And of course specific customs, for example the veiling of women and the insistence on concealing, dark clothing, such as the Iranian chador, must be reinstated to roll back the tides of foreign example and consumerist impulse. The "consumption of what is forbidden" must stop. "It is not merely an evil, but a hideous and most dangerous evil." Iranian revolutionaries quickly reinstated legal requirements for traditional dress, and in the process chador-clad women shouted against their sisters in Western dress, calling them "European dolls" and "prostitutes."

The rise of Islamic fundamentalism and its influence, not only in Iran but also in leading secular regimes such as Turkey, Algeria, and Egypt, was not of course the final word. Interests in consumerism persisted as well. We have seen that commitments to stylish, Western-oriented dress actually increased in Turkey in the last two decades of the twentieth century. Egypt remained a center for genuinely Middle Eastern, but also consumerist film production, with impact throughout the region. It was the ongoing division that was striking, as each side fed the other. Consumers knew they were making a statement of values, beyond their interest in specific fashions or goods. Fundamentalists knew that while their power was considerable, they had not definitively won the day. A debate over identity continued, and the forces of what the fundamentalists viewed as "cultural pollution" remained strong.

Consumerism had emerged both slowly and distinctively in the Middle East, particularly amid the Muslim majority. The process reflected the strength of the traditional and religious alternatives. Ultimately, the extent of change was impressive as well – which is why a new round of opposition emerged, surprisingly late by standards elsewhere in the world but striking in its focus. The result was a region where consumerism's future was unusually unclear at the outset of the twenty-first century, precisely because the debate remained so vivid and active. The choice of consumerism, for those who made it amid doubts and despite potential opposition from family and friends, was more than a material one. Here was a key similarity to other instances in consumerism's world history, where symbolic meanings often overshadowed any shallow indulgence. What was unusual, as the twenty-first century dawned, was how contested the choice might still be, and how many people still explicitly sought an alternative to consumer values.

Further reading

Pre-twentieth century: Eliyahu Ashtor, *Levant Trade in the Later Middle Ages* (Princeton, NJ: Princeton University Press, 1983); Ross Dunn, *Resistance in the Desert: Moroccan Responses to French Imperialism, 1881–1912* (London: Croom Helm; Madison: University of Wisconsin Press, 1977); Fatma Gocek, *Rise of the Bourgeoisie, Demise of Empire: Ottoman Westernization and Social Change* (New York: Oxford University Press, 1996); Roger Owen, *The Middle East in the World Economy 1800–1914* (London: Methuen, 1981).

On the twentieth century: John Esposito, *The Iranian Revolution: Its Global Impact* (Miami: Florida International University Press; Gainesville: University Presses of Florida, 1990); Imam Khomeini, Hamid Algar, trans., *Islam and Revolution* (Islam: KPI, 1981); Annabelle Sreberny-Mohammadi and Ali Mohammadi, *Small Media, Big Revolution: Communication, Culture and the Iranian Revolution* (Minneapolis: University of Minnesota Press, 1994); Oslem Oz, *The Competitive Advantage of Nations: The Case of Turkey* (Aldershot, Hants; Brookfield, VT: Ashgate, 1999); Donald Quataert, ed., *Consumption Studies and the History of the Ottoman Empire, 1550–1922* (Albany: State University of New York Press, 2000); Elizabeth Thompson, *Colonial Citizens: Republican Rights, Paternal Privilege, and Gender in French Syria and Lebanon* (New York: Columbia University Press, 2000); Subidey Togan, *Foreign Trade Regime and Trade Liberalization in Turkey During the 1980s* (Aldershot, Hants; Brookfield, USA: Avebury, 1994).

Part III

Consumerism toward the new century

The two chapters in this final section discuss very recent trends in international consumerism, with examples from several societies but with emphasis on the increasingly elaborate global apparatus, and they offer a concluding evaluation.

Consumerism continues to involve change and innovation, even in the West. New kinds of protests and counterreactions emerge as well, but as the twenty-first century dawned, some of the contours of consumerism were well established, even in many societies outside Western Europe and the United States. So it is important to look for continuities as well.

Thus specific advertising techniques and themes changed. In many societies, the use of sexual overtones to sell goods increased, as permissiveness expanded in the wider culture. But there were familiar themes as well. Many advertisers still tried to link goods to self-improvement and to family well-being. Even as women's roles shifted, consumer pitches continued to emphasize their family expertise, as against bumbling husbands. But masculinity sold other goods, such as cigarettes.

Even the very rich often replicated spending patterns first established by the upper class of a century or more before: thus amid growing upper-end affluence in the United States, the very wealthy emphasized familiar items such as elaborate mansions and even yachts, where sales zoomed upward.

Variations among societies reflected earlier cultural patterns also. Advertising in Japan, with strong traditions of gender differentiation, could emphasize masculinity far more than its counterpart in Scandinavia, where feminism had established an early foothold.

Ongoing trends, then, reflected a phenomenon that was well established though still debated. More of the same, rather than decisive new patterns, describes many aspects of consumerism at the beginning of the twenty-first century. The unprecedented new international linkages, though they too built on earlier patterns, represented the clearest change. Vehicles such as MTV provided a near-universal consumer language for young people from California to Israel and on to Japan. Though still in infancy, on-line purchases over the Internet were possible across national boundaries and in defiance of national laws that might attempt to ban such items as Nazi paraphernalia. Novel communications technology blended with the maturing of consumer interests in a host of otherwise different societies.

And, with the tentacles of consumerism still spreading, it is vital not only to offer a snapshot update but also a stab at assessment. The final chapter looks briefly at some of the leading historical patterns, as modern consumerism neared its three-hundredth birthday. It particularly raises issues of evaluation, ultimately asking (but not pretending a definitive answer) whether consumerism has improved or deteriorated the human experience.

Chapter 12

Consumerism in the contemporary world

Consumerism at the end of the twentieth century featured four kinds of developments. First, changes within individual societies marked some new ramifications. We will select examples here, looking first at the West, then at some additional cases, pointing to an acceleration of consumerism in many areas. Second, new or renewed resistance to consumerism developed. This included the revived vigor of Islamic reaction, discussed in the previous chapter, but also religious and other protest movements elsewhere – even in the West. Classic forms of hostility to consumerism faded, particularly with the decline of fascism, but there were important new objections. The third theme was the most obvious story: the emergence of a more extensive international network for consumerism, based on new technologies, the extension of multinational business operations, and a growing audience for consumer interests in many parts of the world. This was what marked the later twentieth century as a new phase in the history of consumerism overall, though the origins lie somewhat earlier. But international consumerism also roused objections, adding to the complexity of the whole phenomenon even as many consumer institutions and behaviors seemed well established. Finally, the fourth theme – perhaps the most important – involved the clearer emergence of various regional styles of consumerism, blending Western models and international standards with local components.

The advance of consumerism in major societies

Western Europe and the United States

It is hard to determine if the final decades of the twentieth century constituted a new period in Western consumer history, or just an amplification of well-established trends. New levels of prosperity in Western Europe, after the post-World War II recovery, certainly brought innovations. Working-class people gained secure access to the world of consumerism for the first time, even though their incomes usually lagged behind those of the middle class. Purchase of motor scooters and then automobiles was one indication. So was access to the increasingly ubiquitous television set, which rapidly became the most popular leisure device throughout the Western world. Many people talked about the working classes becoming bourgeois because of their commitment to consumerism (a process called *embourgoisement*). Relatedly, some of the classic working-class protest forms receded in importance, in part because workers were too busy enjoying their lives as consumers or working overtime to pay for them. The West European peasantry also became more interested in sharing in consumer gains. The old passion for spending largely on acquiring more land receded.

In the United States and Europe alike, there were important changes in the apparatus of consumerism. Television permitted a huge increase in the impact and ubiquity of advertising. In Europe, state control of television modified this potential for a while, but by the 1980s commercial TV had gained ground rapidly; and in the United States, television and advertising went hand-in-hand from the outset. The ability to stimulate consumer demands on the part of young children went up, thanks to television. The department store, that classic consumer institution, gave way increasingly to the mall, particularly in the United States, which expanded the physical space and variety available to consumerism. Many people began to cruise malls simply as a leisure time activity. But this was clearly a modest redefinition of consumer interests, not a fundamental change. Product linkage involved another new marketing device, as a new movie would have tie-ins to toy lines and fast-food giveaways. Catalog sales and purchases from the Internet were other significant expansions of consumer potential. One could now buy from the comfort of one's own home, usually twenty-four hours a day.

There were some interesting modifications of earlier consumer interests and behaviors, quite apart from the steady multiplication of potential purchases with the proliferation of must-have products ranging from hula-hoops or Game Boys to expansion of vending machines. In the United States, for example, men began to manifest some of the same interest in appearance-enhancing items that once defined female consumerism. By the 1980s and 1990s, male interest not only in clothing, but also in cosmetics and hair dyes and in cosmetic surgery rose rapidly. Style assertions and consumer thefts extended to such items as athletic shoes, which in turn became steadily more elaborate and expensive.

Consumer motivations may have expanded, just as advertisements became more alluring. One historian interprets the growing fascination of upper-middle-class Americans with huge homes ("McMansions") and traditional-style furniture as a reaction to increasingly rapid geographic mobility. People are trying to recapture a sense of roots by buying older trappings – even though their lifestyles permit them to spend little time in their huge homes.

Some observers argued that the most fundamental change in Western, and particularly American, consumerism involved the extension of consumer behaviors to areas of activity not previously considered part of consumer life. Politics was one. Electoral candidates were increasingly packaged like consumer products. They chose their policy positions, emotional style, and even their clothing on the basis of careful market research. Political consultants were essentially marketing and advertising agents, and their role in the campaign process expanded steadily. To be sure, some campaign managers complained that their clients were a bit difficult in the early days. A California expert noted:

> An automobile is an inanimate object; it can't object to your sales talk ... A candidate, on the other hand, can and does talk back ... We have the problem of ... his willingness or unwillingness to hew to the line of the plan of strategy that has been worked out ... his ability or inability to measure up to the character you give him by your carefully-prepared build up.

But while a few candidates objected to the whole process – "the idea that you can merchandise candidates for high office like breakfast cereal ... is the ultimate indignity to the democratic process" – they quickly fell in line. As early as the 1950s American campaigners were buying short television spots and hiring advertising agencies such as a firm famous for its "I Dreamed I Went Walking in My Maidenform Bra" campaign. By the 2000 presidential campaign, key candidates were changing their shirt colors to match what pollsters told them their image should be, and while European campaigns moved to the American style gradually, they too took on an increasingly commercial air.

Consumerist attitudes spread to higher education, again particularly in the United States. A variety of business consultants began to urge that students be called, and treated like, customers, and students and their parents often agreed. They were capable of arguing that since they were paying money for education, they deserved not only good treatment but also good results. Painful processes like posting grades for everyone to see were made illegal; no one should suffer publicly. Grade levels themselves steadily inflated, lest feelings be hurt. Courses and professors were regularly rated, just as motels were. These changes had many merits; but they unquestionably showed the power of consumer expectations and procedures to spill over to other aspects of life.

Consumerism affected art and memory. While some artists continued to attack debased or "philistine" consumer taste, others eagerly produced for a consumer market, such as the sidewalk artists appealing to the tourist trade in major Western cities. Some high-fashion artists also began to incorporate consumer products, such as soup cans or ketchup bottles, into their own production, from the 1960s onward. Particularly fascinating was the growth of consumerism associated with visits to museums and tourist sights. By the

1970s, museum stores began to expand rapidly, and many people spent more time picking out consumer mementoes of a visit than they did in the visit itself. An experience might not seem authentic unless it yielded a related purchase that could be taken home and shown around. By 2000 Americans were buying over $1.5 billion worth of souvenirs, and other societies were not far behind. In some cases people bypassed the tourist site in favor of going directly to the store. Beaches sold sand in a bottle; Kentucky offered figurines made out of turd. The important thing was to have something to buy.

Some critics contended that even marriage became a consumer game for some people. With half of all marriages ending in divorce in the United States, and a third in Great Britain, some marriage partners clearly viewed their spouse in consumerist terms. Commitment was fine as long as the product gave pleasure, but when this lessened one could always trade in on a new model. With the rapid decline of the birth rate after the 1960s throughout the West, family life increasingly revolved around shared consumer purchases and consumer leisure, with marriage convenient largely because two wage earning spouses enhanced buying power. A new breed called "yuppies," or young urban professionals, defined success in terms of an elaborate consumer lifestyle.

Consumer labels began to be attached to every conceivable location. Stadiums and professorships were named by paid sponsors. Political conventions proudly acknowledged their financial backers from the corporate world of goods and services. On a more personal level, wearing a pair of pants might be enhanced if it had its designer label clearly attached, so that walking down the street became an advertisement. Clearly, the distinction between consumerism and non-consumer activities began to disappear.

Consumerism intruded steadily into sports arenas, including the Olympic Games. By 2000, athletes were at least as likely to emphasize some new consumer product, touted by a sports equipment manufacturer, as their national affiliation.

Developments in Western consumerism in the late twentieth century constituted a steady evolution, punctuated by an occasional dramatic new product or marketing device. Each new step seemed logical, because the commitment to consumer goals was by this point deeply rooted. It simply seemed normal to many people, in many different arenas, to view life through a consumer lens and to have almost every facet of life graced with a consumer label.

For many people, particularly in the United States, the commitment to consumerism introduced a new precariousness to material life. By 2001, despite unprecedentedly high incomes, over half of all Americans had almost no savings and a third lived paycheck to paycheck, often in considerable consumer debt. In some cases this situation reflected continued real poverty, but in others it followed from a sense that so many goods and trips had become absolutely essential.

Outside the West

A number of societies made big jumps toward fuller consumerism in the final decades of the twentieth century. Israel was a case in point. This new nation had long been devoted to Jewish identity in a hostile environment. Collective farms sought to shape a communal existence for many people. But by the 1980s and 1990s, consumerism diverted many Israelis from primary concentration on these staples. Cities such as Tel Aviv were filled with consumer lures, and the more religious Jews tended to concentrate in other places such as Jerusalem. Many young people abandoned the communal farms because conditions were too stark, or insisted on introducing individual consumer items such as television sets.

A larger, consumer-oriented middle class developed, along with the growth of cities and considerable industry, in countries such as Mexico and India. Even though poverty levels remained high, consumer items spread surprisingly widely. The very rich, of course, had long indulged consumer tastes, and this opportunity continued. Shopping trips by wealthy oil tycoons from the Middle East or large landowners from Latin America to the luxury stores of London, Paris, or Miami were legendary. The expansion of a consumer middle class was the more novel development. By 1990 twenty-two percent of all Brazilians owned cars, fifty-six percent had television sets, and sixty-three percent had refrigerators. By the same date, India boasted a growing middle class, and while their consumer interests were not quite as honed as those of their counterparts in Latin America, they too displayed an appetite for various kinds of consumer goods. Gandhi's vision of an India devoted to traditional crafts while avoiding Western-style consumerism in favor of spiritual and nationalist goals had clearly receded. New urban spaces created comfortable settings for tourists and consumption-minded young people, complete with transistors blaring rap music and surrounded by shops.

India's middle class was estimated at between 85 and 170 million people, about 20 percent of the population consuming half of all goods. What one observer called the "craze for goods" in this group accounted for considerable disdain for the desperately poor majority, and a new interest in emigrating to the West for higher-pay jobs. But even within India, purchases of refrigerators, motor scooters, and cars escalated rapidly (by 1000 percent between 1970 and 1987), while locally produced films regularly showed scenes of even greater luxury. In India as in Latin America, intensifying consumerism not only created new barriers with the very poor, but also began to dismantle the policy of import substitution, for the new consumers demanded goods of higher quality, which often meant foreign imports.

Indeed, a key economic strategy in many parts of the world involved emphasizing regional consumer goods industries, in areas such as clothing and automobiles, that could satisfy the growing market at home without requiring expensive imports from the West. We have seen that elements of this import substitution strategy developed in the 1920s and 1930s, but acceleration occurred in the final third of the twentieth century. Thus India and Turkey set up their own automobile brands, for the national market. In Latin America, European companies established regional factories with much the same effect. Volkswagen in Mexico continued producing the classic Beetle long after it had been taken off the new-car market in Europe and the United States. Here and elsewhere, consumer expansion occurred despite massive poverty and continued struggles over industrial development.

By the 1990s even some of the more remote parts of the world began to accept a new level of consumerism, though tentatively. A few spots, such as North Korea and Myanmar (Burma) remained largely closed, desperately poor but also eager to protect a non-consumerist communist or Buddhist culture. However, they increasingly stood out as exceptions. The land-locked Himalayan nation of Bhutan, for example, cautiously decided to allow television at the end of the 1990s. The local station produced a few shows of its own, but largely offered fare imported from Europe, Japan, and the United States. Officials believed that careful screening would prevent frenzied consumerism; they had no desire to weaken devotion to community and Buddhist values. But they had clearly decided not to try to keep consumerism out entirely. It remained to be seen whether degrees of involvement could be rationed.

Another symptom of the international growth of consumerism involved a global epidemic of obesity. The United States led the way, with huge weight gains from the 1980s onward. But weight zoomed up in Europe and among middle classes in China and India as well – particularly among children. Growing delight in foods designed as consumer items – snacks and rich coffee drinks, for example, combined with sedentary work and leisure surrounded by consumer products such as computer games. Accelerating consumerism was changing the human body.

Anti-consumer protests

Some of the classic reactions against consumerism declined by the late twentieth century. It was no longer fashionable to berate the working classes for wanting goods above their station. Some elitists might still believe this, but it had become risky to be so blatantly undemocratic. The masses could still be criticized for bad taste, but not for consumerism in itself. The same shift reduced attacks on women as frivolous consumers. Concern about women did inform Islamic fundamentalism, but in most regions of the world a sense that consumerism suggested some special weakness on women's part lost validity. Consumer interests were too widespread to single out any one group. Fascist appeals to traditional dress largely disappeared with the movement itself, and obviously communist alternatives to consumerism declined as well.

These important changes did not mean that consumerism had silenced its opponents, or that consumers themselves now felt guilt-free. Religious appeals increased in vibrancy in many parts of the world from the 1970s onward. They might not be explicitly anti-consumerist, but they certainly urged that consumer issues be given low priority. Newly-fervent movements developed not only in Islam, but also in Christianity with the rise of fundamentalism in the United States, parts of Latin America, and even Eastern Europe, and in Hinduism and Buddhism as well. Hindu nationalists, for example, loudly protest the spread of beauty pageants, arguing that "In India, women are not meant to be sold. Women are not treated as a commodity available for sale in the bazaar." Linked to religious revival, many groups might voluntarily return to traditional dress, as with the spread of head scarves among Muslim women in places in Egypt: it was more important to protect customary identity than to keep pace with the latest fashions.

Explicit attacks on consumerism developed in the West. Student protest in the 1960s involved a strong countercultural current that sought to develop alternatives to consumer goals. Hippies and other countercultural groups scorned many of the trappings of consumerism. The goal was a more natural existence. Many communes were established that shunned commercial purposes and emphasized a simple standard of living in which personal relationships, not things, would hold pride of place. Flower children attacked the work-to-consume rat race. The counterculture ultimately faded, though individuals continued to seek a rural alternative to consumerism and a few communes survived. Many former hippies joined the ranks of consumers. Elements of the counterculture turned out to be convertible to consumer products. Less formal, brightly colored clothing, treasured by the counterculture, was after all a consumer item. Rock music turned out to be eminently commercial.

A fascinating, if modest, effort at consumer control in the United States involved moves to require school children to wear standardized uniforms, rather than individual and potentially enviable or disruptive consumer products. The effort suggested some very old motives of display regulation, though in practice it did not advance very far.

A more durable moral and political counterweight to consumerism involved the rise of new levels of environmental concern in many parts of the world but particularly in the West and Japan. Consumerism took a clear and growing toll on the environment. The sheer amount of non-biodegradable garbage generated by high-consumption societies, headed by the United States, created obvious environmental problems. So did gas-guzzling cars. By 2000, with less than five percent of the world's population, the United States was consuming over 30 percent of the energy resources and creating pollution to match. Not all of the growing pollution problems could be laid directly at the door of consumerism; sheer population expansion and growing industrialization in nations such as China played a role as well. But environmentalists urged appropriate political and personal controls on the consumer impulse, in the name of natural beauty and the survival of the planet. "Green" movements gained great support in countries such as Germany and Holland, around efforts to curb consumer excess. Even aside from politics, the environmental movement created new opportunities to express (or ignore) guilt about affluence. Children could criticize consumerist parents for failing to sort their trash properly; adults could feel just a bit better about their self-indulgence when they took the trouble to find the neighborhood recycling bin.

Environmental protest did not really slow consumerism overall. Some people loudly rejected environmental constraints, like the many Americans who felt that driving cars that consumed large amounts of gasoline was part of their birthright. Green movements failed to catch on in some places, for example France, to the same extent as in some neighboring countries. But the movement persisted, with the potential to organize new anxieties about consumerism in the future. Environmental concerns motivated much of the new protest against globalization, and therefore global consumerism.

Outside the West, many intellectuals lamented the rise of consumerism and the inroads on local cultural identities. The theme of identity against consumerist pressures defined the work of many writers from Japan to Mexico.

Concern also continued about the impact of Western consumerism on local cultures as well as the local economy. The rapid spread of international commercial tourism from the 1950s onward plus an avid market for "exotic" craft imports affected traditional styles. African craft workers, for example, began to modify their expressions in order to match up with what Westerners thought African art should look like. Workers in tourist industries often ignored the behavior of their clients when they went home after work, but the lures of different styles of dress and consumer behavior could tempt some away from customary decorum and family discipline. Again, there was ample room for attacks on consumer-led erosions.

By the late 1990s, international corporations and global economic policies drew a new surge of protest. Meetings of international economic agencies such as the World Bank were greeted with angry crowds of environmentalists, youth, and labor groups, in meetings in the United States and Europe. Representatives of poorer countries joined the attack. A French farmer became a hero when he attacked a local McDonald's outlet, tearing down the golden arch sign. Protests against McDonald's surfaced elsewhere. More generally, Europeans turned against genetically altered foods in the 1990s, refusing to buy imported American meats and grains and insisting on new levels of government protection.

Even within the United States, and certainly elsewhere, concerns about health and local vitality could spur new protests. Books such as *Fast Food*

Nation called attention to the drawbacks of the consumer diet in the United States; protests against chains such as Wal-mart featured hostility to their reliance on cheap foreign labor and their ability to displace local businesses.

These new currents expressed a range of anxieties about the new global economy, and they involved more than consumerism. Workers feared competition from low-wage areas; poor agricultural countries wanted more help from the industrial powers. But there was a strong consumer element as well. Many consumers worried about losing control over the goods they purchased and the identities they maintained, to faceless international corporations. They wanted some protection from the barrage of foreign cultural imports. Here too was an old concern about consumerism, but now directed to the international economic framework amid new protest forms. Emotions could run high.

The global apparatus

It was the international framework itself that witnessed the greatest innovations in late-twentieth-century consumerism. More and more corporations learned how to market consumer goods and services internationally. More and more people prided themselves on a consumer cosmopolitanism, taking goods and services from all parts of the world and integrating them into a consumer lifestyle.

New technologies speeded acquaintance with consumer patterns elsewhere in the world. By the late twentieth century, over a quarter of the world's population might watch the same show on TV (such as World Cup soccer) at the same time – an unprecedented experience. Export, mainly from the West, of popular movies and shows, as well as consumer outlets such as fast-food restaurants, offered another link. Travel was vital. Individual students would come to Western Europe or the United States, usually for technical training, and might also learn consumerism, to take back home. Larger migrations of workers – for example, Turkish workers to Western Europe after World War II – provided another source of new ideas, as they kept in contact with friends at home. Tourism, particularly from the West and Japan, could bring awareness of new styles and values to ordinary people in resort areas. International resorts sprang up almost everywhere the climate permitted, expressing a new, global quest for pleasure; chains such as the European-based Club Med featured standard water sports and cuisine, with a modest bow to local attractions. Their activities mainly affected the global tourists themselves, but they could have some local impact. Even military action played a role in global consumerism – American soldiers spread awareness of consumerism wherever they went. American military presence in Kuwait in the 1990s, for example, helped inspire new shopping malls and a growing interest, against Muslim custom, in tight jeans and cosmetics. By the same token, we have seen that reactions against cultural change often included efforts to limit international contact in the name of threatened local styles and beliefs.

American movies and TV shows helped lead the way in international consumerism. By the 1970s, they stood in second place among American exports, with only aircraft ranking before them. Consumer leisure forms in themselves, American movies and shows also showed the whole world the American consumer lifestyle, prompting often eager response. We have seen that the internationalization of movies began early. By the early 1920s American films controlled 95 percent of the Australian market, and loomed almost as large in Latin America. Americans were seen as holding the secret of making films that appealed to the masses, and glamorizing a middle-class, youthful consumerist lifestyle was part of this secret. United States films gained over European offerings in the Middle East because they were cheaper and more action-oriented. Hollywood became the international movie capital, shaper of international images of beauty and sexuality, from that point onward. The later surge of slickly-produced American TV shows simply intensified this trend. American pop culture icons such as Britney Spears served as international beauty standards, inspiring imitation in fashion and cosmetics from Russia to Madagascar.

Other institutions attached themselves to the emergence of the world's first international popular culture, based around consumerist leisure and imagery. Beauty contests spread, from their origin in the United States in the 1920s. Within the United States, ethnic groups, such as Chinese Americans, began to sponsor shows to demonstrate that they too shared the national lifestyle. Foreign competitions gained ground, featuring women who displayed fashionable bodies but also promoted stylish clothing, music, and other consumer attributes. Products associated with movies won international appeal. Disney figures such as Mickey Mouse attached children to international consumerism with toys and T-shirts.

The spread of McDonald's was another American-derived symbol of international consumerism, touting unfamiliar food products such as the hamburger and an unusually rapid eating style accompanied by ever-smiling service. McDonald's began in Illinois, in 1955, building on the precedent of smaller fast-food chains. The company catered to the traditional American interest in eating fast, adding a family atmosphere and typical American food products. International expansion came quickly, first in Canada and Puerto Rico in 1967. From that point to 1988, the company entered an average of two new countries a year, and then speeded up in the 1990s. By 1998 it operated in 109 countries overall. Western Europe, New Zealand, and Australia were obvious targets, though McDonald's and its American counterparts and local look-alikes surprised observers with their success in traditional centers of gourmet cuisine such as France. By 1990, 26 percent of all restaurant meals in France occurred in fast-food outlets, with youthful eaters leading the charge. The company won quick success in Japan, where it gained its largest foreign audience; "makadonaldo" first opened in Tokyo's world famous Ginza, already known for cosmopolitan department stores, in 1971. McDonald's entry into the Soviet Union, in 1990, was a major sign of the ending of Cold War rivalries and the growing Russian passion for Western consumer goods. The restaurants, which had to organize special training to create smiling personnel, won massive patronage despite (by Russian standards) very high prices.

The parade of international consumer goods was a long one. Barbie dolls won a global audience. T-shirts with real or imagined American university labels were all the rage. American-style Christmas trappings, including gift giving, caught on not only in countries of Christian origin, such as France, that had not previously celebrated the holiday commercially, but also Muslim Istanbul. Northern Mexico picked up American Halloween trick-or-treating, though elsewhere the more religious celebration of All Saints' Day held firmer. Lower-caste youth in India, when money permitted, began to wear blue jeans and T-shirts labeled with words such as "boss," developing a local vocabulary to explain why these items were the height of cool fashion and the good life.

Consumer internationalization was not just American. Japanese rock groups, soap operas, and comic animation won worldwide audiences, including in the United States. The Pokémon toy series, though derived from Japanese cultural traditions, won a frenzied audience among American children-consumers, who just could not get enough. European consumer products and icons spread widely. Finland led the world in the production, and per capita use, of cell phones, a work-related consumer essential by the early twenty-first century. American consumerism routinely included a host of European and Japanese products, as well of course as foods, raw materials, and manufactured clothing and furniture from literally all over the world. McDonalds spread widely internationally, but so did Italian and Chinese restaurants. Many areas mixed American and other products fairly indiscriminately. Thus while American movies were widely shown on television stations in the more secular societies of the Middle East, so were Japanese soap operas, and many local viewers adopted favorite heroes and heroines from both sources. South Korea, though historically hostile to Japan, proved open to Japanese rock music groups and cartoon animation, which caused some consumers to rethink their antagonism to Japan more generally. India's television Channel V, a counterpart to MTV, features mainly Filipino, Japanese, Indian, and some Arab pop music, though introduced by ethnic Indian disk jockeys raised in North America or Britain who mainly speak English. The American lead in international consumer style-setting was crucial, but the blending of influences was vital as well.

Cultural combinations

Consumer internationalization was of course modified by regional influences, blending the foreign with the familiar. This is a standard pattern amid significant cultural contact, and it certainly applied to consumerism. Though less showy than outright globalization, this blending, or syncretism, was arguably the most important development as consumerism became a global standard by the twenty-first century. Blending allowed old and new influences to mix, and permitted a bit of hesitation about consumerism to be combined with modern consumerism itself.

Thus India watched some Hollywood movies, but it also developed the world's largest center of film production based on its own traditional epic stories; there was no wide export, but a strong national presence. Bollywood movies used Indian themes and widely-heralded Indian stars, but with Hollywood production values and a mixture of Western and Indian dress. Hong Kong became a major production headquarters for Asia, and Egypt and Russia formed other major film centers catering to regional demand. McDonald's offered standard products worldwide, but it had kosher products in Israel (McDavid's); a teriyaki burger in Japan; and vegetarian dishes in India (where in any event its popularity lagged). The McDonald's in Rabat, Morocco, served traditional fare after sundown during Ramadan. Holiday greeting cards spread as part of Ramadan, traditionally a period of denial; but they were combined with traditional rituals and piety.

The Mexican comic book provided a classic case of how international consumer interests could be modified in favor of local tastes, creating a distinctive amalgam. Comic books were imported to Mexico from the United States as early as the 1930s, and they caught on fast in a situation where literacy was not uniformly high. Comics were quickly modified to accommodate Mexican standards of beauty and also political values. Thus one series noted: "He was no vulgar bandit, he shared with the poor who live under the lash of vile capitalism," while another touted the hero: "It is the story of a noble, audacious and very Mexican man who struggles against injustice, aiding the social class he came from." Macho exploits were touted, but there was also greater emphasis on kinship and community ties than in United States comics. Indeed, Mexican heroes were often pitted against United States characters such as the "Invincible Jack Superman of Indianapolis," and the gringo characters lost out every time. By the later twentieth century, comic books were far more regularly read in Mexico than in the United States, for they had come to fill a distinctive national cultural space, blending the popularity of American styles with additional ingredients.

Beauty contests in India spread widely, particularly after an Indian woman won a "Miss World" competition in the mid-1990s. Dozens might occur within individual cities, to the dismay of course of full traditionalists. But the contests normally also included displays of traditional dress and local foods and cultural products. One ambitious syncretic venture admittedly went too far: a group in Kerala, a South Indian state, tried to sponsor a contest in which young women would combine beauty with knowledge of Keralan language and customs. The problem was that the people who wanted to compete in such contests didn't know the traditions – they assumed this was just another pageant, while the traditionalists wanted nothing to do with even syncretic contests. But the larger point remains: advancing consumerism in India was inspired by foreign models in part, but also merged with recognizable symbols.

The result, in this case and many others, was a definitive change. People in many countries were attracted to increasingly similar products, particularly when they were linked to the increasingly international communications media. The styles of the richest countries were widely influential, and the sense of sharing in global patterns was attractive as well. But the result was not absolute global uniformity, as different regions adapted consumerist values to more familiar standards.

Even Western Europe featured a different consumerism, by the later twentieth century, than did the United States. Again, there were hosts of shared motivations, products, and styles. But Europeans devoted more resources to public amenities and particularly to leisure than did their American counterparts. Their vacation time expanded rapidly, to five weeks or more by the later twentieth century, whereas American leisure if anything declined somewhat amid growing pressure to work. The American passion for large houses, however, was not matched in Europe. And Europeans were much less heavily involved in credit card debt than were Americans, whose obsession with acquiring consumer objects by this point led the world.

This capacity to combine consumerism with distinctive, often traditional interests was a tribute to consumerism's triumph around the world: it was both necessary and worthwhile for people with sufficient means to accept the new force but also to make it recognizable. But the same pattern suggests that it was becoming essential to talk about different specific consumerisms, and to explain why they emerged within the larger, more obvious global framework.

Further reading

J.R. Rabier, *Consumer Attitudes in Europe 1975* (Ann Arbor, MI: Interuniversity Consortium for Political and Social Research [distributor], 1978); Grant McCracken, *Culture and Consumption: New Approaches to the Symbolic Character of Consumer Goods and Activities* (Bloomington: Indiana University Press, 1988); Don Slater, *Consumer Culture and Modernity* (Oxford, UK: Cambridge, MA: Polity Press; Blackwell Publishers, 1997); Mary Douglas and Baron Isherwood, *The World of Goods: Toward an Anthropology of Consumption* (London; New York: Routledge, 1996); Maggie Andrews and

Mary Talbott, eds, *All the World and Her Husband: Women in Twentieth-Century Consumer Culture* (London; New York: Cassell, 2000). On India: Carol Breckenridge, ed., *Consuming Modernity: Public Culture in a South Asian World* (Minneapolis: University of Minnesota Press, 1995); Robert Stern, *Changing India: Bourgeois Revolution on the Subcontinent* (Cambridge, UK; New York: Cambridge University Press, 1993); Rajni Kothari, *Poverty: Human Consciousness and the Amnesia of Development* (London: Zed, 1993); Amartya Sen, *Commodities and Capabilities* (Delhi; New York: Oxford University Press, 1999). On Latin America: Duncan Green, *"The Silent Revolution": The Rise of Market Economics in Latin America* (London: Cassell; New York: LAB; distributed in North America by Monthly Review Press, 1995); Alan Wells, *Picture-tube Imperialism? The Impact of U.S. Television on Latin America* (Maryknoll, NY: Orbis Books, 1972); Benjamin Orlove, ed., *The Allure of the Foreign: Imported Goods in Postcolonial Latin America* (Ann Arbor: University of Michigan Press, 1997). On internationalization: James Watson, ed., *Golden Arches East: McDonald's in East Asia* (Stanford, CA: Stanford University Press, 1998); Stephen Rees, *American Films Abroad: Hollywood's Domination of the World's Movie Screens from the 1890s to the Present* (Jefferson, NC: McFarland, 1997); Theodore von Laue, *The World Revolution of Westernization* (New York: Oxford University Press, 1987).

Chapter 13

Conclusion

Who wins – consumerism or consumers?

History answers several basic questions about consumerism – for example, why did it get started, and how do different societies vary? It defines other questions that require more personal evaluation. This chapter highlights the major issues.

The development of consumerism represents one of the great changes in the human experience, literally around the world, over the past two or three centuries. The emergence of new types of marketing and advertising is important in itself, as part of modern economic history. But it is the shift in behavior and personal expectations that is really intriguing. Large numbers of people have come to define life somewhat differently, and have fostered new kinds of hopes and frustrations accordingly.

This is a recent development, as big historical shifts go, but already it has a complex history. Far more is involved than the apparent simplicity of shopping and acquiring.

While consumerism shows the power of change – a key focus for historical inquiry – it also shows the importance of historical continuities. Each major society has received and elaborated consumerism a bit differently. Key historical factors involved in this distinctive shaping include prior social structures and their degree of rigidity, and of course gender relationships and assumptions as well. The cultural context is also crucial. Consumerism gains ground more smoothly when the prior culture was heavily secular. But even secular philosophies like Confucianism condition the experience. Government involvement can be critical as well; different political traditions have encouraged different levels of state policy to promote, channel or discourage consumerism. The power of consumerism is obvious. Its appeal has often allowed it to advance despite various political, cultural and social obstacles, but the power does not run roughshod over history, which is why international consumerism is not a uniform product.

History also reminds us of crucial differences in timing. Some societies are "farther along" in consumerism than others, and the differences here may prove durable. The historical record also makes it clear that consumerism never progresses unopposed, and that it may even be slowed or temporarily reversed. At the outset of the twenty-first century, powerful objections to consumerism persist in many parts of the world, and we may see new cases in which the consumer apparatus is rolled back. We will certainly see vigorous debate over the phenomenon almost everywhere, though the specific forms will vary from one society to the next.

The importance of variations in the receptions of consumer behaviors may seem unexpected, for it is tempting to look at consumerism as a uniform phenomenon, some undifferentiated product of Westernization. But the variations are real, and they continue to shape consumerism's prospects.

History also explains why consumerism exists at all, though the balance among factors must still prompt debate. The apparatus is one element from the first: consumerism exists partly because so many clever people promote it, with increasingly sophisticated techniques, but consumerism also exists because it meets other needs. Its role in responding to blurrings of identity is crucial. Consumerism helps people deal with confusions about social status and with challenges to established patterns because of new foreign influence. Consumerism also, relatedly, allows quiet challenges to hierarchy, in terms of social class, gender, even parental authority. It provides some sense of freedom and individual expression, however superficial the outcome. And, particularly outside the West, it offers a sense of belonging to a larger whole, of gaining access to the up-to-date and modern. It compensates for change, and also provokes further change in the interests of apparent personal fulfillment and new forms of identity. Finally, of course, consumerism takes increasing root with time, unless (rarely) it is successfully rolled back by effective opposition. People come to grow up with consumerism from infancy; they assume its logic and normalcy.

The combination of three components – manipulation, fulfillment of social and personal needs, and habituation – serves as consumerism's incubator and ongoing support. Shopping may offer some intrinsic pleasures, but there are reasons for its growing role in human life.

History does not, of course, tell us exactly what comes next, and important issues surround consumerism's future. Three question marks particularly apply to consumerism's prospects as the twenty-first century moves forward. The first involves the impact of the religious revival affecting many regions of the world, from Islam, to a new movement in China derived in part from Buddhism, to the surge of Protestant fundamentalism in Latin America, to the increased popularity of religious commitments in the United States. Religious fervor can of course coexist with consumerism, but there are inevitable tensions. Will religion provide an alternative to consumer interests, and if so where, and to what extent? To what extent do the fervent religions take hold particularly among people – the urban unemployed, for example – left out of consumerist gains, and to what extent do they inhibit consumer interests?

The second issue involves the new surge of protest against multinational corporations and global trade policies. This protest led during the year 2000 to unexpectedly vigorous demonstrations against international economic agencies such as the World Bank, in cities ranging from Seattle to Geneva. The protest does not focus on consumerism per se, but it does argue that protecting jobs and the environment should take precedence over maximizing consumer gains. It also involves groups that do disavow consumer goals outright, harking back to the alternative spirit of the 1960s. Where will this lead? Is it possible that either local or global protests will displace consumerism?

The third issue, related to both the others, involves the growing economic gap that has opened worldwide between the relatively affluent and the increasingly poor. The gap has widened steadily during the past two decades. It involves certain regions, like much of Africa, in disproportionate poverty, at levels that inhibit consumerism of any sort. It also involves left-out groups even within the United States, that have found their incomes stagnating or falling as income inequality becomes sharper. For the poor, consumerism is not the question; seeking adequate subsistence is. The question haunts a large percentage of people in Africa, South Asia, and elsewhere. It haunts the growing number of children below the poverty line – thirteen million in the year 2000 – in the United States. Where will the growing inequality trend lead? Will it generate new forms of protest, or will it simply continue to create a divide, within societies as well as internationally, between those who can and those who cannot significantly participate in modern history's new toys? There is an additional twist. Many poor regions and poor people now provide low-wage labor to make consumer goods for others. Long hours and unsafe conditions add in as well. This includes sweated peasant workers in China, making Christmas ornaments or firecrackers, workers making fashionable sneakers in Vietnam, textile workers in Indonesia or Lesotho. Spreading consumerism, and the quest for low prices and greater profits, in this sense contributes directly to poverty, to the great divide between those involved in the system and those left out.

Again, it is essential to assume debate and constraints when contemplating consumerism's future prospects. Some issues are new – environmentalism, for example, at its current level of concern – but complexity has long been part of consumerism's impact.

Still, for all the question marks, it is logical to assume that consumerism will continue to gain ground, as more societies seek to share in the presumed delights. China, for example, clearly seems poised for greater consumerism, and Russian interest is obvious though clouded by uncertain economic prospects. Large middle classes in countries such as India, Mexico, Turkey, and Brazil already define life in part through standard consumer acquisitions. Many other groups and regions seek larger slices of the consumer pie. Even in the United States, amid some questions about whether unprecedented affluence provides enough purpose in life, consumer interests continue to surge forward. Indeed, economies from the United States to China, and to some degree globally, now depend on steady and advancing consumerism. Small wonder that consumer diligence has come to be virtually an obligation of citizenship, particularly in the United States, essential to keep the wheels of society turning. American leaders, urging a return to normalcy after the terrorist attacks of 2001, made the point clearly: "keep buying and keep flying."

The steady intensification of consumerism – despite problems and despite real inequalities – leads to three final questions that focus on evaluation of consumerism's meaning and impact rather than on historical perspective and forecasting alone. First, is consumerism making the world too homogeneous, at undue cost to regional identities and expressions? Second, will the spread of consumerism usher in other historical changes, and of what magnitude? And third, wherever it has hit or will alight, is consumerism a good thing, in terms of human values?

The homogeneity issue goes to the core of a world-historical approach to consumerism, but it is not easy to deal with. The spread of consumerism does involve convergence on shared goals and many shared styles. To take a simple point: people around the world dress more similarly, at the outset of the twenty-first century, than ever before since clothing was invented.

T-shirts, blue jeans, neckties are everywhere. Consumerism encourages people to seek minor individual variants in clothing – a distinctive slogan on the T-shirt, for example – but amid great, growing, and often truly international conformity.

Indeed, we have seen that one of the goals of consumerism, particularly outside the West, has been a sense of participation in a larger global community. People even accept products they don't greatly like, such as McDonald's fare, in order to gain this sense of belonging, in order to shake off a sense of parochialism and separateness.

Yet homogeneity is far from complete. People continue to differ over consumerism, as a result of the wide disparity in earnings but also because of very different expectations. The rural-urban gap still shows in most societies. Rural people stake more on acquisition of land and family solidarity than their urban cousins do, and work less strenuously to maximize consumer gains. Different societies offer distinctive packages as well. The tensions between consumerism and community traditions in Africa are not felt to the same degree in Japan. Partly this reflects differences in historical timing, but there may be more involved. Japanese consumerism is associated with individualism to a degree, but it has not erased a far greater sense of conformity in Japan than in the West. Europeans spend far more on vacations and vacation time than Americans do, a huge difference in the definitions of appropriate consumerism even within the West. Americans lead the world in personal credit card debt, reflecting a particular addiction to maximizing consumer opportunities as early as possible (or, according to concerned critics, earlier than is really possible). There is no reason to believe that the rest of the world will follow this American example, for again precise goals continue to vary by group and region. Many Indians embrace aspects of consumerism, but they also combine it with local fashions.

In other words, consumerism does erase some divisions and it does create unprecedentedly wide interest in some common types of items, even single brands such as McDonald's or Mickey Mouse or Pokémon. It does permit people to find known consumer emblems virtually everywhere they travel. It does encourage a sense of global belonging. But it does not erase all differences. Whether the world's peoples are becoming too similar around consumerism, or whether too many differences still hamper mutual understanding remains an important tension. Consumerism has not eliminated the tension.

A second question about consumerism, both past and future, involves range of impact. We have seen that consumerism can affect more than buying habits and personal and family life. Many people believe it has profoundly altered the political process in countries such as the United States, leading to new levels of manipulation in "selling the candidate." But as consumerism deepens, and spreads to still more countries, will there be further effects? One American journalist, Thomas Friedman, in his book *The Lexus and the Olive Tree*, argues that deeply consumerist societies will not wage war against each other. He contends that when lots of people in a society enjoy the fruits of consumerism, they no longer want to go to war, and so war will decline (except, of course, for aggrieved societies where consumerism has not yet taken hold). He notes the unpopularity of military service in many consumerist societies. This is an ambitious theory, and frankly not enough time has passed to judge whether it is right or wrong. (Consumerist England eagerly went to war against Argentina in the 1980s over the Falkland Islands, but of course it was a minor engagement, and also Argentina was not yet fully consumerist, so maybe the theory didn't apply.) But thinking this way about the potential precedent-shattering effects of global consumerism at least points the way to the possibility of wide impacts on our future. The United States attack on Iraq, in 2003, shows that deeply consumerist societies will still go to war when they can be persuaded they are under threat. But the war (like the Vietnam war before it) was also intriguing in that it did not call for significant consumer sacrifice; taxes were not raised and people were encouraged to keep on spending, as government deficits mounted. Perhaps Friedman should be modified: consumerist societies will prefer wars that do not interfere with consumer life, but other goals may take precedence and drive them to battle despite consumerism. And if this is so, how much has this aspect of history really changed?

More basically still: is consumerism "good?" In one sense the question is unanswerable except in terms of personal values, and people clearly disagree. Consumerism can be appallingly shallow. It opens even thoughtful people to manipulations by salesmen and advertisers. It does relate to a decline of spiritual values and other intangibles. It does generate mindless conformities. It may even make people less aware of their own emotional reactions, as they seek to buy yet another item that will distract them. It certainly can reduce protest, making people reluctant to confront social injustice or deteriorations at work so long as their buying power holds up. It can negatively affect the environment, by encouraging unregulated production and creating wasteful products.

But consumerism can be defended, even without denying some of the criticisms. New goods provide new levels of comfort and diversion, and arguably even beauty, into ordinary life. Few people would willingly go back to pre-consumerist material standards – though this may reflect the extent to which consumerism has blinded them to higher values. It is also true that some commentary on consumerism, still today, reflects elitist disdain for the pleasures of the masses and a related sense that the lower orders should not call attention to themselves. It often assumes that ordinary people don't know what's good for them – which is possible but not certain.

It is also vital to recognize how consumerism has often stood for goals and concerns well beyond material acquisition. We have seen that consumerism gives many people a sense of global belonging. It also often stands for freedom and individual choice. This was true in the past and remains true for many today. It often stands as well for an attack on rigid social or gender hierarchy. These strivings through consumerism may be disapproved of, as elite critics have often done when consumer gains challenged hierarchy. Or consumerism may be attacked for serving the goals badly; freedom, for example, may be a goal in consumerism that is thwarted by conformity and commercial manipulation. But a judgment of consumerism must recognize its important service to broader social and personal interests. It is not always as shallow as it seems. Many people express themselves through it, in ways impossible in earlier times.

What of the loss of identity consumerism may involve? Consumerism and Westernization are not the same thing, in that some societies, for example those of Japan or Africa, may increase consumerism without totally surrendering to Western values. Outside the West, consumerism has always involved an attack on regional traditions through attraction to imported goods and tastes. This may not only offend nationalist pride, but also seriously disorient individuals who voluntarily commit to consumer goals. They may end up – as some Africans claim to feel – not knowing who they are.

Even in the West, it is hard to say whether consumerism has made people happier. Measuring happiness historically is terribly hard, perhaps impossible. Clearly, the advance of consumerism has always involved losses as well as gains, and some of the drawbacks have not been clearly perceived by enthusiasts. One study, issued in 2000, claims that major consumer gains in a society – a real move upward in material standards – initially causes a definitive jump in measurable happiness. But after that and in more established consumer settings, consumerism is irrelevant to claimed satisfaction, and people enmeshed in milder forms of consumerism may be happier than consumerist zealots.

The study of consumerism in world history does not provide a definitive balance sheet on whether the long-term results are favorable or unfavorable. But it does provide perspective, allowing greater understanding of what consumerism involves, and perspective, in turn, offers a greater capacity to choose an appropriate level of involvement, rather than being swept away by the latest enthusiasm.

Understanding where consumerism comes from, what needs and pressures it responds to, does not prove that consumerism is good or bad. But historical understanding does generate some opportunity for considering one's own take on a truly powerful international force in contemporary life. It also helps to know what some of the criticisms have been, and to be able to compare one set of national patterns against another.

Managing consumerism is a challenge, for it is easy to be managed by it. But consumerism is a human construction, despite all the complex factors behind it. It should serve human ends.

Index